CCNA Voice Portable Command Guide

Robert M. Cannistra
Michael Scheuing

Cisco Press
800 East 96th Street
Indianapolis, IN 46240

CCNA Voice Portable Command Guide

Robert M. Cannistra & Michael Scheuing

Copyright © 2013 Cisco Systems, Inc.

Published by:
Cisco Press
800 East 96th Street
Indianapolis, IN 46240 USA

Printed in the United States of America 1 2 3 4 5 6 7 8 9 0

First Printing January 2013

Library of Congress Cataloging-in-Publication data is on file.

ISBN-13: 978-1-58720-442-5

ISBN-10: 1-58720-442-8

Warning and Disclaimer

This book is designed to provide information about network security. Every effort has been made to make this book as complete and as accurate as possible, but no warranty or fitness is implied.

The information is provided on an "as is" basis. The authors, Cisco Press, and Cisco Systems, Inc., shall have neither liability nor responsibility to any person or entity with respect to any loss or damages arising from the information contained in this book or from the use of the discs or programs that may accompany it.

The opinions expressed in this book belong to the authors and are not necessarily those of Cisco Systems, Inc.

Trademark Acknowledgments

All terms mentioned in this book that are known to be trademarks or service marks have been appropriately capitalized. Cisco Press or Cisco Systems, Inc. cannot attest to the accuracy of this information. Use of a term in this book should not be regarded as affecting the validity of any trademark or service mark.

Corporate and Government Sales

The publisher offers excellent discounts on this book when ordered in quantity for bulk purchases or special sales, which may include electronic versions and/or custom covers and content particular to your business, training goals, marketing focus, and branding interests. For more information, please contact:

U.S. Corporate and Government Sales
1-800-382-3419
corpsales@pearsontechgroup.com

For sales outside of the U.S. please contact:

International Sales
international@pearsoned.com

Feedback Information

At Cisco Press, our goal is to create in-depth technical books of the highest quality and value. Each book is crafted with care and precision, undergoing rigorous development that involves the unique expertise of members from the professional technical community.

Readers' feedback is a natural continuation of this process. If you have any comments regarding how we could improve the quality of this book, or otherwise alter it to better suit your needs, you can contact us through e-mail at feedback@ciscopress.com. Please make sure to include the book title and ISBN in your message.

We greatly appreciate your assistance.

Publisher
Paul Boger

Associate Publisher
Dave Dusthimer

Managing Editor
Sandra Schroeder

Project Editor
Seth Kerney

Editorial Assistant
Vanessa Evans

Cover Designer
Gary Adair

Composition
Jake McFarland

Business Operation Manager, Cisco Press
Anand Sundaram

Senior Editor
Mary Beth Ray

Development Editor
Eleanor C. Bru

Copy Editor
San Dee Phillips

Technical Editors
Dave Bateman
Ralph Smith III

Proofreader
Chuck Hutchinson

About the Authors

Robert M. Cannistra is a full-time faculty member at Marist College located in Poughkeepsie, NY, where he teaches networking, voice communication, security, wireless communication, and system administration courses within the School of Computer Science and Mathematics. Outside of teaching, Robert provides network consulting services for enterprise, service provider, and medical organizations for network design, configuration, and troubleshooting.

Robert has held the positions of Northeast Regional Manager, Technical Services Manager, and Senior Consultant for a Cisco Gold Partner. His time there was spent designing, configuring, and implementing highly accessible data networks for various enterprise, service provider, and Internet companies across the world; some of those clients included Quaker Oats, Milwaukee Electric Tool, AC Nielsen, Cogent Communications, and EthnicGrocer.com, among numerous others. Upon the completion of each client implementation, he would develop and instruct customized training courses to help the client manage the newly designed networks. Robert has taught as an adjunct faculty member at Rensselaer Polytechnic Institute (RPI) for their Computer Science, Engineering, and Information Technology curricula and as an adjunct technical instructor for a technical institute in Poughkeepsie, NY. He has also held the positions of Senior Network Engineer for About.com, Inc., Internet and Intranet Infrastructure Webmaster at AT&T Solutions, and Systems Engineer at Kodak Imaging Services.

Robert holds a master of science degree in Computer Science/Information Systems, a bachelor of science degree in Computer Science, an associate of science in Liberal Arts and Science, and several industry technical certifications including CCAI, CCNA, CCSP, MCSE, CLP, and several others.

Whenever Robert has a free moment (which isn't very often), he enjoys spending time with his wife, Kara, two sons, Luca and Rylan, and their dog, Tripster (a coonhound who always stands right behind him and his wife so they take full advantage of her name...as they trip over her).

Michael Scheuing has witnessed the evolution of Cisco voice products since first working on Call Manager 3.1 many years ago. Drawing upon 15 years of telephony and network experience, Michael has designed, implemented, and maintained voice and data infrastructures for small businesses and large enterprise alike.

Michael currently works as a Telecommunications Engineer responsible for the architecture and management of a complex voice and video network consisting of legacy PBXs, Cisco Unified Communications Manager, and Cisco TelePresence.

About the Technical Reviewers

Dave Bateman, CISSP, GFSP, GAWN, CHS-IV, CGEIT, ECSA, C-EH is an industry veteran with 20 years of experience covering information security. Most recently Phil was one of the very few Senior Technical Solutions Architects at Cisco Systems focused on Data Center and Security. Phil's areas of expertise include sanctioned Attack and Penetration, Digital and Network Forensics, Wireless Security, Network Security Architecture, and Policy work. Phil is also an Adjunct Professor at St. John's University in Queens, NY, teaching Wireless Security to all levels of undergraduate students. Phil earned his MS-CIS (Cyber Security) from Boston University in 2009 and is a frequent information security show speaker and trusted advisor to many large firms.

Ralph Smith III, CCIE No. 15412, is a systems engineer education specialist for Cisco Systems. His focus is on security technology and training development. James has more than 18 years of experience in IP internetworking, including the design and implementation of enterprise networks. Prior to joining Cisco Systems, James provided Cisco training and consulting for Fortune 500 companies and government agencies. He holds two bachelor's degrees from University of South Florida and is currently working on his MBA at The University of Tampa.

Dedications

Robert M. Cannistra: To my wonderful and amazing family: my wife, Kara, and our two boys, Luca and Rylan. Without their love, encouragement, support, laughter, and smiles, I don't know what I would do.

Kara, you truly are an absolutely wonderful person and I'm so thankful to spend my life with you! Thank you for always maintaining a positive attitude and bringing happiness to everyone around you!

Luca, you are one of a kind—don't ever let that trait get away from you! You make me smile, laugh, and are teaching me so much as you grow.

Rylan, you are pure joy! You make me smile, laugh, and help maintain the child within me.

Michael Scheuing: I dedicate this book to my loving family, Doris and Paola, in thanks for their unending support, understanding, and love throughout the many hours of writing and editing.

Acknowledgments

Robert M. Cannistra: Words cannot describe how grateful I am for Mary Beth Rays' patience with this project. Life has its twists and turns. Her warm heart, calming nature, and helpfulness throughout this project made this book possible. I can't thank you enough!

Michael Scheuing, this wouldn't have been possible without you! Thank you for all your work, commitment, and knowledge!!

Ellie Bru, your editorial comments helped tremendously! So, thank you for all your hard work!

Chris Cleveland, we ran into problems from day one and you were there to help see us through them, so thank you!

Dave Bateman and Ralph Smith, thank you both for your helpful technical edits and keeping us on the ball!

Mom and Pop, thanks for all of your guidance and support throughout my life. You truly are the best parents!

Nick and Karen, thanks for always being there and for your unbiased support.

Margie, God rest your soul! You were a true inspiration growing up! We love you!

Dave, God rest your soul! You were like a second father to me! You are truly missed!

And thank you for the team behind the scenes at Cisco Press in making the manuscript come to life.

Michael Scheuing: I would like to thank my co-author, Robert Cannistra, for the opportunity to collaborate on this book with him. Robert's enthusiasm for the topic was contagious and his expertise helped to shape this book, making it current and relevant.

To Dad and Carol, thank you for your support and love throughout it all.

To Mom, thank you for believing I could do anything.

To my brother Rob who helped me to learn what it takes to succeed and inspired me to push myself further than I thought possible. Your business philosophy and work ethic is something I continue to use every day.

To Nino: "It's gotta be done!"

To the technical editors, thank you for your thoughtful feedback and expert guidance.

Finally, I would like to thank the team at Cisco Press, especially Ellie and Mary Beth for their help, motivation, and for keeping us focused.

Contents at a Glance

Contents

Icons Used in This Book

Workgroup Switch
Voice-Enabled

Network Cloud,
White

Cisco Unity
Server

IP Telephony
Router

File/Application
Server

Cisco Unified
Presence Server

PC

Cisco
CallManager

Network Cloud,
Gold

IP Phone

Workgroup
Switch

Voice-Enabled
Router

Cell Phone

Phone

Command Syntax Conventions

The conventions used to present command syntax in this book are the same conventions used in the IOS Command Reference. The Command Reference describes these conventions as follows:

- Boldface indicates commands and keywords that are entered literally, as shown. In actual configuration examples and output (not general command syntax), boldface indicates commands that are manually input by the user (such as a show command).

- Italics indicate arguments for which you supply actual values.

- Vertical bars (|) separate alternative, mutually exclusive elements.

- Square brackets [ ] indicate optional elements.

- Braces { } indicate a required choice.

- Braces within brackets [{ }] indicate a required choice within an optional element.

Introduction

Welcome to CCNA Voice! This *Portable Command Guide* was written to help give you another resource to utilize as you prepare for the CCNA Voice exam. While this book was designed to provide details for task-oriented and step-by-step administrative functions, it is not intended to be your only source of information for CCNA Voice. The step-by-step nature of this book provides the background information to help you further understand the material you learn.

We think that once you earn your CCNA Voice certification you will find yourself referring to this book as you administer your Cisco voice products. Since the book covers a wide variety of topics with examples as well as hints and tips, it could be a valuable resource for years to come as well!

Who Should Read This Book?

Whether you are studying for the CCNA Voice certification exam 640-461 ICOMM (Introducing Cisco Voice and Unified Communications Administration) v8.0 or just want to dive into the configuration of a Cisco Voice and Unified Communications Network, this book will be useful to keep on hand. This book takes a detailed, practical approach to the configuration and implementation of Cisco Unified Communications Manager, Cisco Unified Communications Manager Express, Cisco Unity Connection, and Cisco Unified Presence utilizing Cisco routers, switches, and IP phones.

Readers will obtain the appropriate knowledge to proactively configure, monitor, maintain, and troubleshoot their organizations' Voice infrastructure by utilizing Cisco Voice and Unified Communications CLI and GUI.

I (Robert) have been a consultant and instructor/professor for well over 11 years. Throughout my years of teaching technology, I have found that students learn best by using a mixed theoretical and practical approach. With this approach, students learn the theory behind a particular protocol or technology and then implement it in a practical fashion. This method blends the two primary styles of learning and provides the students with a complete understanding of the technology. This book is meant to be a standalone book in the sense that students and professionals would/could use this book to learn the concepts, the configuration, and the troubleshooting steps necessary for a successful implementation. However, this book can also be used by the professional who needs to simply implement a feature within a small Cisco Voice solution. This book is also a helpful supplement to the *CCNA Voice Official Exam Certification Guide*, written by Jeremy Cioara and Michael Valentine, which goes into more theoretical depth on each topic.

How This Book Is Organized

Although you could read this book cover-to-cover, it is designed to be flexible and allow you to easily move between chapters and sections of chapters to cover only the material you need. If you do intend to read them all, the order in which they are presented is an excellent sequence.

Chapters 1 through 9 cover the following topics:

- **Chapter 1, "Voice Fundamentals for Unified Communications":** This chapter provides an overview on voice fundamentals, traditional voice with the PSTN, Cisco VoIP structure, and other protocols used in voice communication.

- **Chapter 2, "Cisco Switch, Router, and Phone Fundamentals for Unified Voice":** This chapter focuses on setting up the foundation for CME utilizing the CLI.

- **Chapter 3, "Cisco Unified Communications Manager Express":** This chapter focuses on the basic operation and configuration of Cisco Unified CME.

- **Chapter 4, "Cisco Unified CME Features":** This chapter focuses on the administration and configuration of several voice features within Cisco Unified CME.

- **Chapter 5, "Cisco Unified Communications Manager (CUCM) Administration and Management":** This chapter focuses on the administration and management of end users and devices in Cisco Unified Manager through the GUI.

- **Chapter 6, "Cisco Unified Communications Manager (CUCM) Telephony and Mobility Features":** This chapter focuses on the configuration and enablement of Telephony and Mobility features within CUCM through the GUI.

- **Chapter 7, "Cisco Unity Connection and Cisco Unified Presence":** This chapter focuses on voicemail integration with Cisco Unity Connection and the configuration of Cisco Unified Presence.

- **Chapter 8, "Management, Monitoring, and Troubleshooting CUCM":**

This chapter focuses on the common issues associated with a Cisco Unified Solutions implementation. Included is managing, monitoring, and troubleshooting CUCM and monitoring Cisco Unity Connection.

- **Chapter 9, "Pulling It All Together":** This chapter pulls the majority of the topics discussed within this book together into one advanced small- to medium-sized business voice network topology demonstrating how these technologies can work together to provide voice communication across a network infrastructure.

CHAPTER 1

Voice Fundamentals for Unified Communication

This chapter provides information on the following topics:

- Voice Fundamentals
- Cisco VoIP Structure
- Common Topologies
- Traditional Voice Network
- Traditional Data Network
- Today's Converged Network

Voice Fundamentals

Over the past decade, as IP-based protocols have matured, a trend has occurred. The trend has been moving away from traditional PBX-based telephony systems and moving toward implementing a converged data and voice IP-based network. This has enabled a lower-cost solution to be deployed over the existing infrastructure that exists for the network.

Whether you have a background in traditional voice, networking, or are new to this field altogether, there are a lot of terms and concepts to learn. The goal for this portable command guide is to help you quickly dive into what you need or want to know to help implement a VoIP solution at work, to help you advance your knowledge to attain the CCNA Voice certification, or simply to further your knowledge in a technology that is foreign to you. Table 1-1 lists commonly used acronyms and concepts with a brief description of each. These terms and concepts are used throughout this portable command guide.

Table 1-1   Voice Fundamentals – Concepts and Acronyms

Acronym/Concept	Description
802.1Q	IEEE Standard specifying a trunking protocol that tags frames with the VLAN number they are sourcing from
Analog Signal	Signaling method used to measure change in a continuous nature
ANI	Automatic Number Identification
CAS	Channel Associated Signaling
CCS	Common Channel Signaling
CDP	Cisco Discovery Protocol
CLI	Command Line Interface
CME	Cisco Unified Communications Manager Express
Codec	Encoding/Decoding mechanism for compressing voice across a data network. The term's original meaning is coder/decoder.
CUC	Cisco Unity Connection
CUCM or CM	Cisco Unified Communications Manager (previously known as Call Manager (CM)
CUP	Cisco Unified Presence
E.164	PSTN International number plan
Digital Signal	A string of bits (1s or 0s).
E&M	(Ear and Mouth) or (Earth and Magnet)
FXO	Foreign Exchange Office
FXS	Foreign Exchange Station
NANP	North American Numbering Plan
NTP	Network Time Protocol
PBX	Private Branch Exchange
PoE	Power over Ethernet
PSTN	Public Switched Telephone Network
RBS	Robbed Bit Signaling
RTCP	Real-Time Transport Control Protocol
RTP	Real-Time Transport Protocol
SCCP	Skinny Client Control Protocol
SIP	Session Initiation Protocol
SRST	Survivable Remote Site Telephony
TDM	Time Division Multiplexing is the process of transmitting multiple channels of voice or data in specific time slots over a single digital connection.

Cisco VoIP Structure

It is beneficial to know what products exist in the Cisco world for voice. Depending upon the size of the organization, numerous solutions are available:

- **Cisco Unified Communications Manager:** This solution is the pinnacle of the Cisco Voice solution. Cisco Unified Communications Manager provides all the functionality you would want or need within an enterprise-class voice solution. This is the ideal solution for a large organization that requires the complexity, yet granularity, of having an enterprise voice system. You can add voicemail functionality to this system when implementing Cisco Unity Connection (CUC). You can also add presence features that will be discussed later within this portable command guide. The presence functionality is known as Cisco Unified Presence (CUP). This is an extremely flexible and scalable solution.

- **Cisco Unified Communications Manager Express:** This solution is for the small- to medium-size business that does not require the complexity, nor the extensive scalability that Cisco Unified Communications Manager has to offer. It is an ideal solution for a small- to medium-size business that would like a subset of the features that CUCM offers. This can also be used for a remote office solution with CUCM utilizing SRST.

- **Cisco Unified Communications Manager—Business edition:** Cisco developed this solution for an organization that wants the full-blown implementation of CUCM; however, the organization will never grow beyond 1,000 users (Note: At the time of this writing, three business editions are available. This is a great solution at a great price point for the small- to medium-size organization.

- **Cisco Unified Communications 500 Series for Small Business (UC500):** Cisco developed this solution for the small business market that just needs a quick, easy to set up and configure platform to get its organization up and running on a VoIP solution. This system scales up to 138 users. This is truly meant for the small business market.

Common Topologies

This section describes common topologies that you find in the industry and in textbooks when studying voice technologies and bridging the gap between data and voice networks.

Figure 1-1 represents the traditional voice network for a traditional PBX connected to the PSTN via a copper ground start trunk or loop start trunk. This also shows traditional phones as terminals and a traditional fax machine, in addition to a connection to the voicemail system.

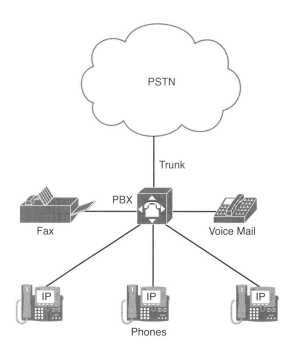

Figure 1-1   Traditional Voice Network

Figure 1-2 represents the traditional data network that shows two locations, each with a router, switch, and two PCs connected via a WAN connection.

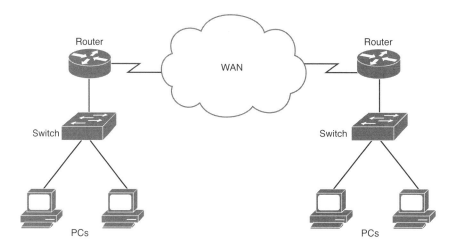

Figure 1-2   Traditional Data Network

Figure 1-3 represents today's Voice over IP network that takes the best of both the traditional voice network and the data network and combines them together in one network. The PBX is now a server on the data network, and the traditional phones are now IP-based. Keep in mind, you still need to maintain a connection to the PSTN for external calls.

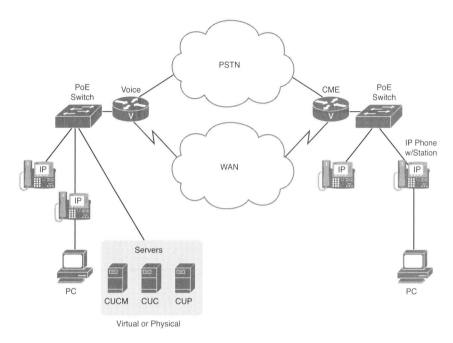

Figure 1-3   Today's Voice over IP Network (Sometimes Referred to as a Converged Network)

CHAPTER 2

Cisco Switch, Router, and Phone Fundamentals for Unified Voice

This chapter provides information and commands concerning the following topics:

- Physically connect the fundamental devices
- Configure the router
  - Hostname
  - Interfaces
    - Physical
    - Subinterfaces
- Configure the switch
  - Hostname
  - MGMT VLAN interface
  - Interfaces
    - IEEE 802.1q trunk
    - Voice only
    - Data only
    - Voice and data
- Resetting the IP Phones to factory defaults
  - Cisco 7965G
- Verification
- Troubleshooting

Technology Overview—Device Connections: Router, Switch, IP Phones

Basic connectivity is the key to a successful implementation, if you work with voice. As you can see from the topology in Figure 2-1, there is a router connected to a PoE switch via a straight-through cable. This connection will be running as an IEEE 802.1q trunk, so be certain to use (at minimum) a 100Mbps/full duplex interface on both the router and the switch. The switch then connects directly to the PCs, or you can connect the PCs through a Cisco IP Phone. The point is to connect the PCs back to the switch in some fashion. If the PCs connect to the switch through the IP Phones, you end up creating and passing two different VLANs on each switch port. In earlier configurations you needed to configure this interface as an 802.1q trunk also; however, in newer configurations you can now pass a Voice VLAN and a Data VLAN over a switchport running in access mode. This is allowed to occur because you are literally separating the voice and data traffic into different types of VLANs. The Administrative VLAN (VLAN 1) is the untagged VLAN; whereas the Data VLAN (VLAN 201) and the Voice VLAN (VLAN 101) are actually tagged with their associated VLAN ID. The configuration prepares the routers, switches, and IP Phones for IP telephony. In the next chapter, you configure the router for IP telephony.

Topology

This section refers to the network topology shown in Figure 2-1 and provides details about configuring the fundamentals for voice.

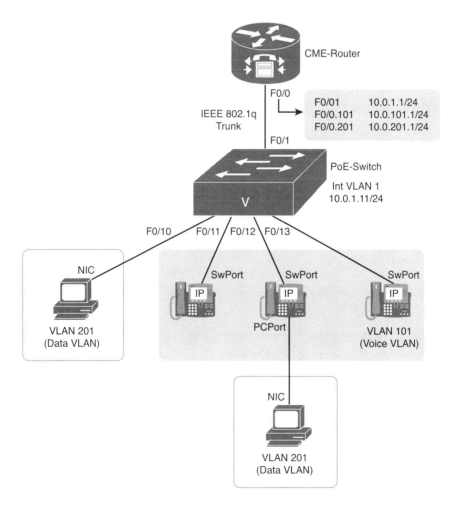

Figure 2-1   Cisco Unified Communications Manager Express Topology

Configuration

Configure the Router's Hostname

Using a terminal emulation program such as putty or securecrt, open a console to the router.

Router#**configure terminal**	Enters Global Configuration Mode of the router.
Router(config)#**hostname** **CME-Router**	Configures the name of the router.
CME-Router(config)#	As you can see, the router prompt changes after the hostname command is entered.

Configure the Router for InterVLAN Routing

NOTE   This is done to support voice traffic and data traffic.

CME-Router(config)#**interface** **f0/0**	Enters Interface Configuration Mode of the FastEthernet 0/0 interface.
CME-Router(config-if)#description IEEE 802.1q Trunk to PoE-Switch for Cisco Unified Communications Manager Express (CME)	Configures a description on the FastEthernet 0/0 interface.
CME-Router(config-if)#**no ip** **address**	Removes any previously configured IP address on the physical interface.
CME-Router(config)#**interface** **f0/0.1**	Enters the subinterface configuration for the MGMT VLAN interface: VLAN 1 in this sample scenario.
CME-Router(config-if)#description MGMT VLAN Interface	Configures a description for this subinterface.
CME-Router(config-if)#**encapsulation dot1q 1**	Sets the encapsulation for the subinterface f0/0.1 to IEEE 802.1q for VLAN 1.
	NOTE The native keyword at the end of this command means that the traffic sourced and destined on this subinterface will not be tagged with the VLAN ID.
CME-Router(config-if)#**ip** **address 10.0.1.1 255.255.255.0**	Sets the IP address of 10.0.1.1 with a subnet mask of 255.255.255.0 or /24.

`CME-Router(config-if)#interface f0/0.101`	Enters the subinterface configuration for the VOICE VLAN interface: VLAN 101 in this scenario.
`CME-Router(config-if)#description VOICE VLAN Interface`	Configures a description for this subinterface.
`CME-Router(config-if)#encapsulation dot1q 101`	Sets the encapsulation for the subinterface f0/0.101 to IEEE 802.1q for VLAN 101.
`CME-Router(config-if)#ip address 10.0.101.1 255.255.255.0`	Sets the IP address of 10.0.101.1 with a subnet mask of 255.255.255.0 or /24.
`CME-Router(config-if)#interface f0/0.201`	Enters the subinterface configuration for the DATA VLAN interface: Vlan 201 in this scenario.
`CME-Router(config-if)#description DATA VLAN Interface`	Configures a description for this subinterface.
`CME-Router(config-if)#encapsulation dot1q 201`	Sets the encapsulation for the subinterface f0/0.201 to IEEE 802.1q for VLAN 201.
`CME-Router(config-if)#ip address 10.0.201.1 255.255.255.0`	Sets the IP address of 10.0.201.1 with a subnet mask of 255.255.255.0 or /24.
`CME-Router(config-if)#interface f0/0`	Enters the physical (parent) interface for all the subinterfaces.
`CME-Router(config-if)#no shutdown`	Enables the physical interface and all the subinterfaces configured within the parent physical interface.

NOTE If more VLANs exist, then you must create additional subinterfaces for each VLAN you are trying to route for.

Configure the PoE Switch for Basic Connectivity

`Switch#configure terminal`	Enters Global Configuration Mode of the switch.
`Switch(config)#hostname PoE-Switch`	Configures the name of the switch.
`PoE-Switch(config)#interface vlan 1`	Enters Interface Configuration Mode of the VLAN 1 interface that will be used for the MGMT VLAN.
`PoE-Switch(config-if)# ip address 10.0.1.11 255.255.255.0`	Sets the IP address of 10.0.1.11 with a subnet mask of 255.255.255.0 or /24 on the logical VLAN 1 interface.

| PoE-Switch(config-if)#no shutdown | Enables the logical interface VLAN 1. |
| PoE-Switch(config)#ip default-gateway 10.0.1.1 | Configures the default gateway for the switch. |

Configure Voice and Data VLANs on the PoE Switch

Configure One Interface for the Data VLAN

PoE-Switch(config)#interface f0/10	Enters Interface Configuration Mode of the FastEthernet 0/10 interface.
PoE-Switch(config-if)#description TO PC0 on DATA VLAN 201	Configures a description for this interface.
PoE-Switch(config-if)#switchport	Sets the interface to a Layer 2 interface. **NOTE** This is required if you config-ure a Layer 3 switch.
PoE-Switch(config-if)#switchport mode access	Sets the switching mode of this interface to access. (This interface will belong to one VLAN.)
PoE-Switch(config-if)#switchport access vlan 201	Assign this interface to the DATA VLAN 201.
	NOTE If the VLAN is not already cre-ated, this command automatically cre-ates the VLAN. There is one stipulation though: The VTP mode of the switch must be running in either transparent or server mode.
PoE-Switch(config-if)#no shutdown	Enables the interface if it is not already enabled.

Configure One Interface for the Voice VLAN

PoE-Switch(config)#interface f0/11	Enters Interface Configuration Mode of the FastEthernet 0/11 interface.
PoE-Switch(config-if)#description TO IP Phone 1 on VOICE VLAN 101	Configures a description for this interface.
PoE-Switch(config-if)#switchport	Sets the interface to a Layer 2 interface. **NOTE** This is required if you are con-figuring a Layer 3 switch.

`PoE-Switch(config-if)#switchport mode access`	Sets the switching mode of this interface to access. (This interface will belong to one VLAN.)
`PoE-Switch(config-if)#switchport voice vlan 101`	Assigns this interface to the VOICE VLAN 101.
	NOTE If the VLAN is not already created, this command automatically creates the VLAN. There is one stipulation though: The VTP mode of the switch must be running in either transparent or server mode.
`PoE-Switch(config-if)#no shutdown`	Enables the interface if it is not already enabled.

Configure One Interface for Both the Data VLAN and the Voice VLAN

`PoE-Switch(config)#interface f0/12`	Enters Interface Configuration Mode of the FastEthernet 0/12 interface.
`PoE-Switch(config-if)#description TO IP Phone 2 on VOICE VLAN 101 AND TO PC2 on DATA VLAN 201`	Configures a description for this interface.
`PoE-Switch(config-if)#switchport`	Sets the interface to a Layer 2 interface **NOTE** This is required if you are configuring a Layer 3 switch.
`PoE-Switch(config-if)#switchport mode access`	Sets the switching mode of this interface to access. (This interface will belong to one VLAN.)
`PoE-Switch(config-if)#switchport access vlan 201`	Assigns this interface to the DATA VLAN 201.
`PoE-Switch(config-if)#switchport voice vlan 101`	Assigns this interface to the VOICE VLAN 101.
	NOTE If the VLAN is not already created, this command automatically creates the VLAN. There is one stipulation though: The VTP mode of the switch must be running in either transparent or server mode.
`PoE-Switch(config-if)#no shutdown`	Enables the interface if it is not already enabled.

Reset the Cisco 7965G Unified IP Phone to Factory Defaults

When a factory reset is completed on a Cisco Unified IP Phone, the CTL file, LSC, call history, and phone application are erased. The user configuration settings, network configuration settings, and locale information are reset to default values.

Step 1: Disconnect either the power cable (if there is one) or the Ethernet cable providing PoE to the phone.	The Unified IP Phone powers down.
Step 2: Connect the power cable or Ethernet cable providing PoE to the phone.	The Unified IP Phone begins the power cycle.
Step 3: When the phone begins to power up, press and hold the # key [SHIFT-3].	**NOTE** You must press this before the speaker button flashes on and off on the phone.
Step 4: When you see each of the line buttons flash on and off in sequence (the color will be amber), you may release the # key. Press the key sequence 123456789*0#.	**NOTE** If you press the sequence correctly, the line buttons flash red. The phone proceeds to the factory reset process. **NOTE** It is acceptable to press a particular key twice, such as pressing the sequence 1123456789*0#. **IMPORTANT** DO NOT power down the phone while the factory reset process is occurring.
Step 5: When the main screen appears, the Cisco Unified IP Phone is now reset to factory default settings.	

Verification

CME-Router#**show version**	Displays the version information. This is required to determine if you have a valid Cisco IOS that supports voice.
CME-Router#**show ip route**	Displays the current routing table. You should verify that you see all directly connected routes for all your VLAN interfaces.
CME-Router#**show ip interface brief**	Displays all your interfaces with their primary IP address and the status of the interface in a quick, easy-to-read, brief overview.

`PoE-Switch#`**`show vlan`**	Displays the current VLAN information, the interfaces assigned to each VLAN, the SAID for each VLAN, and other information.
`PoE-Switch#`**`show vlan brief`**	Displays the current VLAN information, the interfaces assigned to each VLAN, and the status of each VLAN without displaying the SAID and other information such as MTU, and so on.

Troubleshooting

Actively Debug Issues When They Arise

`PoE-Switch#`**`debug vlan`** **`encapsulation-events`**	This command enables you to see if the appropriate frames are encapsulated and deencapsulated properly.

CHAPTER 3

Cisco Unified Communications Manager Express

This chapter provides information and commands on the following topics:

- Topology
- Administration Interfaces
- Implementing Cisco Unified Communications Manager Express with a router utilizing CCP
  - Configuration
    - Configuring Cisco Unified Communications Manager Express for the first time

Topology

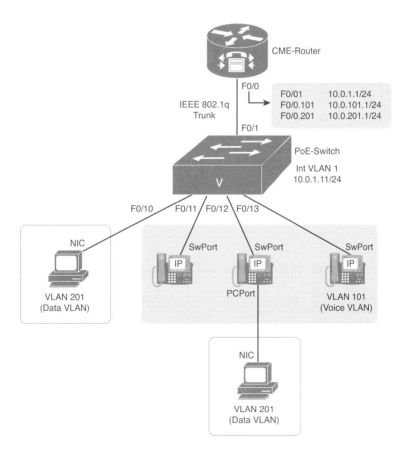

Figure 3-1 Cisco Unified Communications Manager Express Topology

Administration Interfaces

There are three administration interfaces for Cisco Unified Communications Manager Express. Two interfaces are available via web-based GUI, and one is available via the CLI (either through a console session, a Telnet session, or an ssh session).

Cisco is working hard to compete with other vendors by developing more intuitive graphical interfaces to configure its equipment such as routers, switches, security appliances, and so on. In the voice realm, this is also true. Cisco uses a GUI for the primary configuration mechanism of Cisco Unified Communications Manager. Now, Cisco has developed a GUI known as the Cisco Configuration Professional, which can be used to configure the majority of voice features for Cisco Unified Communications Manager Express. This is great for an IT administrator who has various tasks to complete in a short time and is not a Cisco CLI guru. The authors have been designing, configuring, and troubleshooting Cisco networks for more than 15 years; however, quite a number of IT professionals do not have that type of Cisco CLI experience. The CCP does a great job to provide an intuitive configuration interface.

Configuration

This section provides you with a walk-though to configure Cisco Unified Communications Manager Express.

Configuring Cisco Unified Communications Manager Express for the First Time

This section refers to the network topology shown in Figure 3-1 and provides details about accessing and using Cisco Configuration Professional (CCP) to configure Cisco Unified Communications Manager Express for the first time on this router.

> **NOTE** You must download the CCP from cisco.com. The installation program is approximately 150MB. To download CCP from cisco.com, you need a CCO account; however, this can simply be an account that has guest privileges and does not require a Cisco support account number.

Accessing and Using the Cisco Configuration Professional

1. After Cisco Configuration Professional is installed on your computer you should access it by using your Windows Start menu and clicking the Cisco Configuration Professional folder. Then click the Cisco Configuration Professional icon, as shown in Figure 3-2.

> **NOTE** There are two executable files: one for a demo mode version that has three standard devices as Community Members and one executable to be used in a production or lab environment. The nice thing about the demo version is that it enables you the flexibility to see what features are available within three different routers without having the physical equipment in place. The 2921 found within the demo version also

supports the voice features, so if you are just starting with voice, this is a great way to learn what features are supported and what you can configure within CCP for Cisco Unified Communications Manager Express.

Figure 3-2   Click the Cisco Configuration Professional Icon

2. After the CCP loads, it defaults to using Internet Explorer as its default browser. You need to provide the IP address or hostname of the router that you want to connect to along with a username and password, as shown in Figure 3-3. Cisco ships its routers with a default username and password. You may use this to access the router configuration via CCP at this point.

3. After you click **OK**, you see the screen shown in Figure 3-4.

   After you click **Discover** to find and authenticate to the router, you will have successfully discovered the router you intend to configure.

4. To begin configuring the Unified Communications Features within this Cisco router, click the **Unified Communications** folder in the left navigation panel to expand the folder. Click **Unified Communications Features**, as shown in Figure 3-5.

Figure 3-3   Provide the IP Address/Hostname, Username, and Password

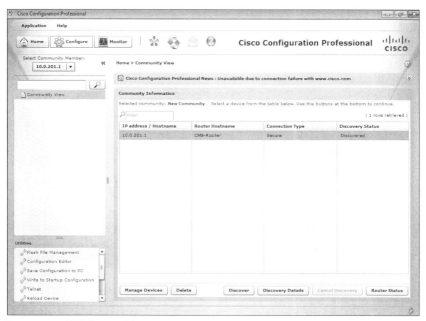

Figure 3-4   CCP Router Discovery

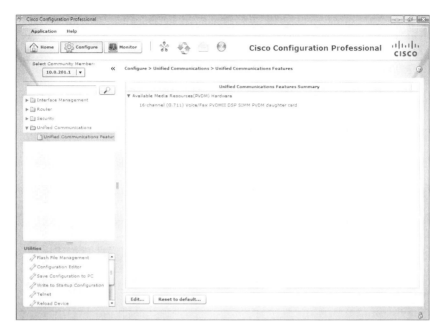

Figure 3-5 Begin Configuring Unified Communications Features

5. Click **Edit** in the bottom-left side of the right navigation panel.

6. Click the **IP Telephony** check box (see Figure 3-7). You have three choices:

    ■ CUCME — Cisco Unified Communications Call Manager Express

    ■ SRST — Cisco Unified Survivable Remote Site Telephony

    ■ Cisco Unified Call Manager Express as Cisco Unified Survivable Remote Site Telephony

    Click the **CUCME** radio button to configure the router as an independent site using Cisco Unified Communications Manager Express. As you can see from Figure 3-6, there are no selections checked by default.

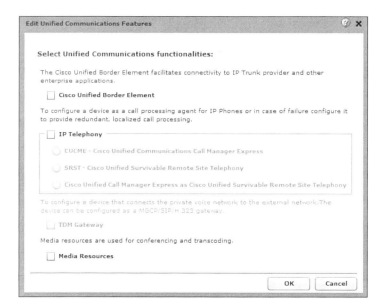

Figure 3-6 Edit Unified Communications Features

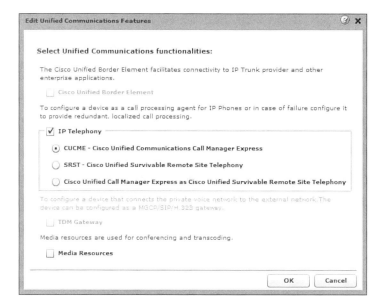

Figure 3-7 IP Telephony Check Box and CUCME Configuration

NOTE After you click the **OK** button, another window appears displaying the CLI syntax (see Figure 3-8). This is extremely useful for a person that is either a novice or an experienced Cisco professional. If you didn't know a command for something, you know it now. Or you can confirm your knowledge of the CLI syntax.

Figure 3-8   CLI Syntax

After you click **Deliver**, the syntax is delivered to the router, and you are now back at the original screen you started at within the Configuration tab, as shown in Figure 3-9.

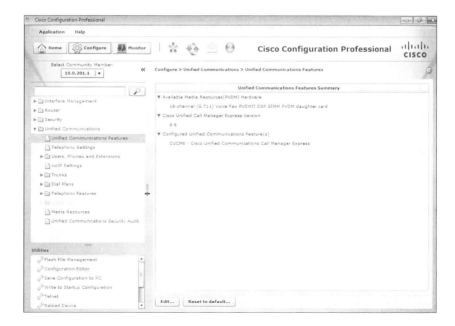

Figure 3-9   Unified Communications Summary

In Figure 3-9 other options have now populated the left navigation panel (other than Unified Communications Features) such as

- Telephony Settings
- Users, Phones, and Extensions
  - Extensions
  - Phones and Users
  - Templates and Firmware
  - Extension Templates
    - Phone Templates
    - Phone Firmware
- VoIP Settings
- Trunks
  - SIP Trunks
- Dial Plans
  - POTS
  - VoIP
  - Translation Rules and Profiles
  - Calling Restrictions
  - Codec Profiles
- Telephony Features
  - After-Hour Toolbar
  - Auto Attendant
    - Basic Automatic Call Distribution
    - Prompts and Scripts
  - Call Conference
  - Call Park
  - Call Pickup Groups
  - Directory Services
  - Hunt Groups
  - Intercom
  - Night Service Bell
  - Paging Numbers
  - Paging Groups
- Voice Mail
- Media Resources
- Unified Communications Security Audit

If you attempt to configure a user extension or other parameter in the left navigation panel below **Telephony Settings**, the informational message states that you must set up the Telephony Service before using one of the other features, as shown in Figure 3-10.

Figure 3-10   Set Up Telephony Service Prompt

You have the basic telephony service configured at this point and are ready to configure other voice parameters.

Basic Telephony Settings

This section refers to the network topology (refer to in Figure 3-1) and provides details about the basic telephony settings you should configure when configuring CUCME using the CCP.

1. From the left navigation panel within the CCP, click **Telephony Settings**, as shown in Figure 3-11. Then click **Edit** in the bottom-left corner of the right con-figuration panel.

Figure 3-11   Click Telephony Settings

Another configuration screen appears, as shown in Figure 3-12.

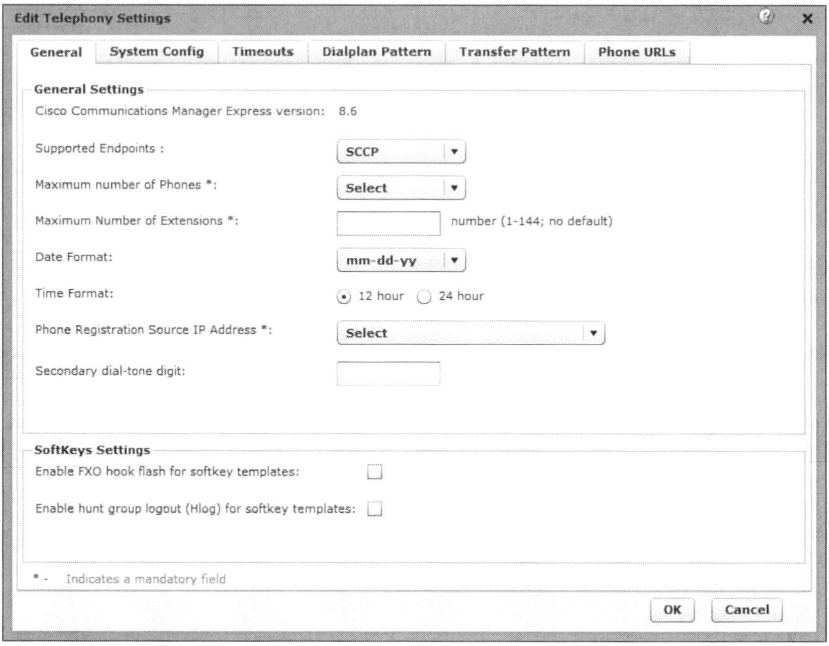

Figure 3-12   Edit Telephony Settings

General Tab

2. On the first tab labeled General, you can find General settings based upon the version of CUCME you are running.

NOTE   At the time of writing this book, version 8.6 is the most current version. Therefore, version 8.6 is used here.

You can notice from Figure 3-13 that there are three options when you click the Supported Endpoints drop-down menu: SCCP, SIP, or SCCP and SIP.

3. If you click the maximum number of phones from the drop-down menu, you can see a few different options depending upon the licensing you have in place on your router, as shown in Figure 3-14.

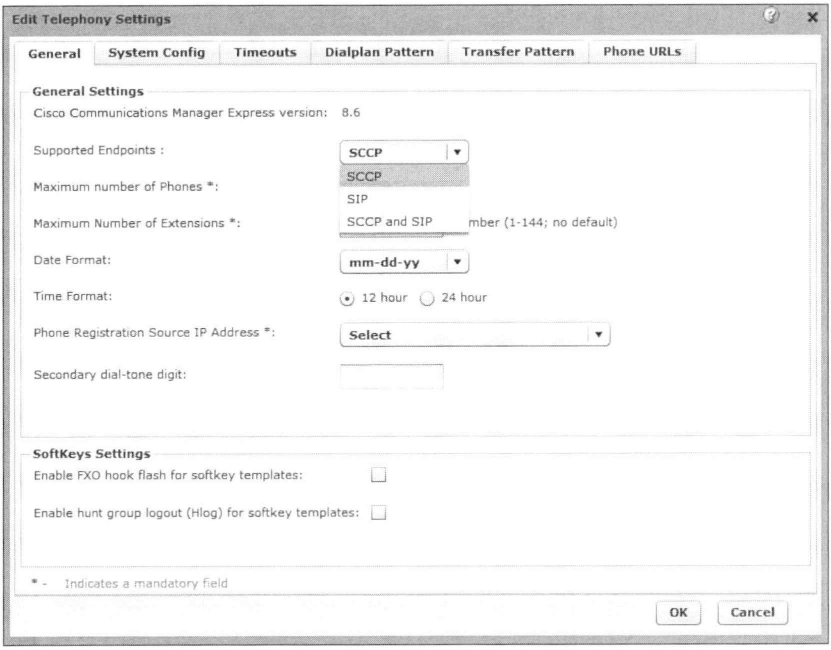

Figure 3-13   There Are Three Supported Endpoints: SCCP, SIP, and SCCP and SIP

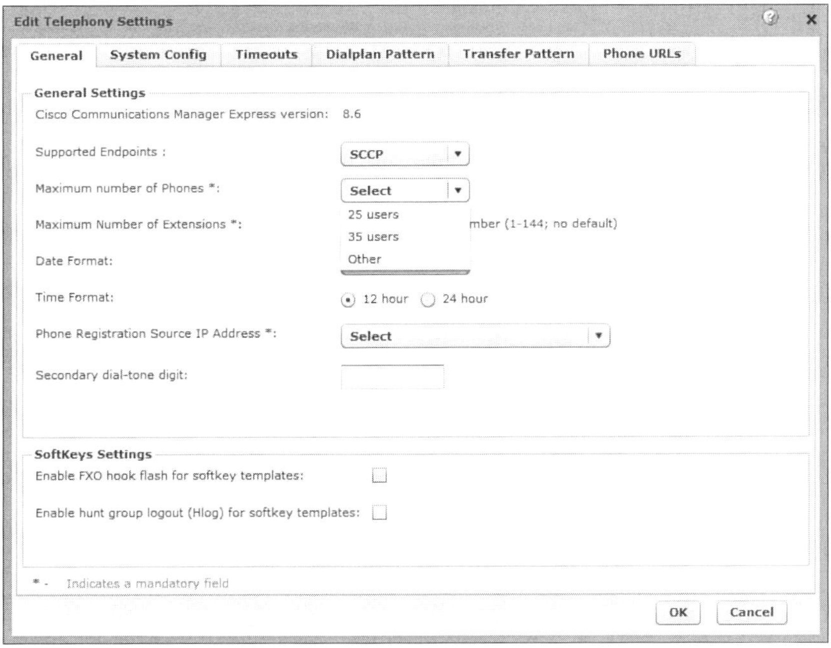

Figure 3-14   Telephony Settings – Maximum Number of Phones Supported

Notice, if you click **Other**, you may specify another value, as shown in Figure 3-15.

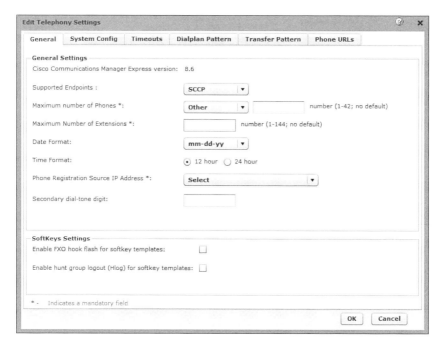

Figure 3-15   Telephony Settings – Maximum Number of Extensions Supported

4. When you click in the field for the Maximum Number of Extensions, you may enter any numeric value up to 144, as shown in Figure 3-16. (Again, this number is dependent upon the licensing you have in place on your CUCME router.)

5. When you click in the Date Format field, you can find the standard four formats used throughout the world (see Figure 3-17).

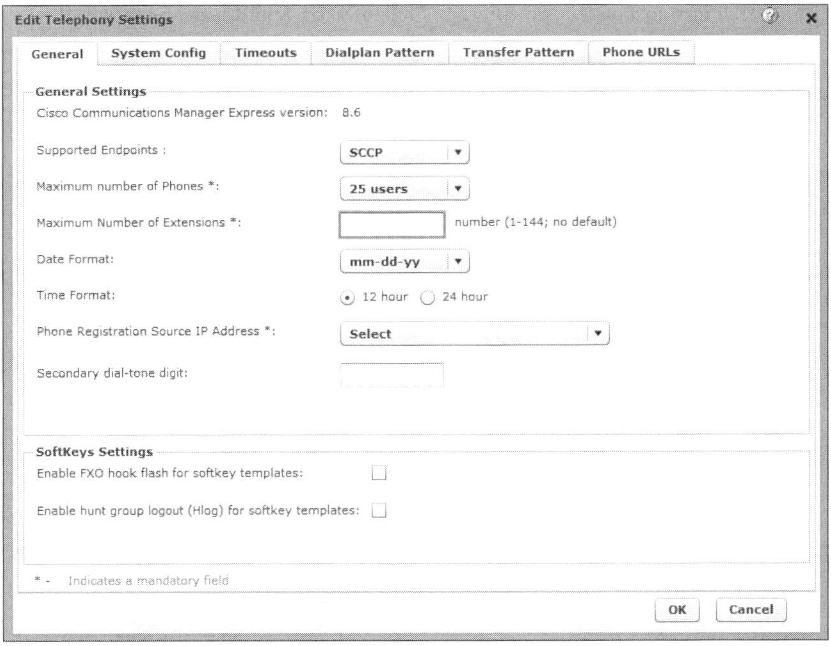

Figure 3-16 Maximum Number of Extensions Field

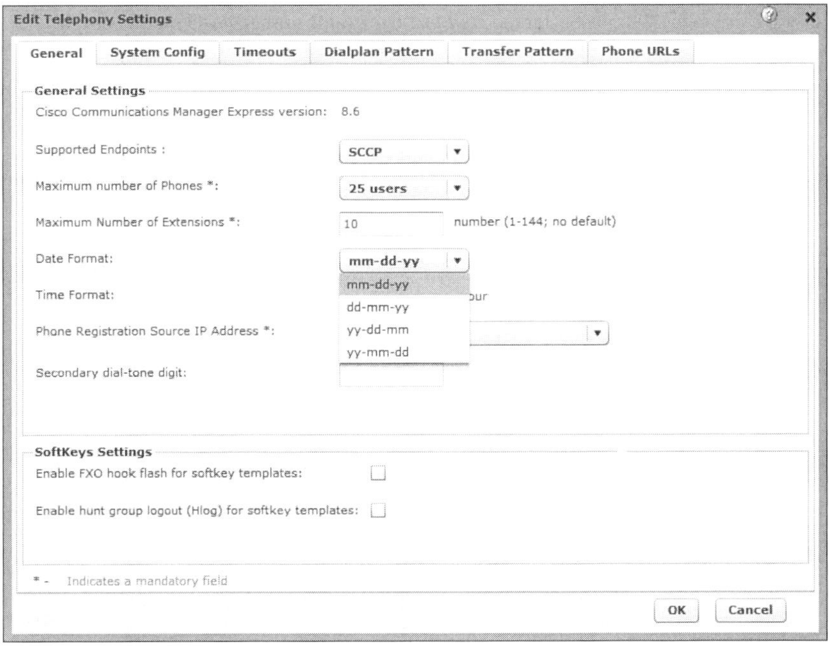

Figure 3-17 Date Format Field

6. When you click in the Time Format field, you can find the two standard time formats: 12 hour and 24 hour.

7. The next field represents what the source IP Address will be for phone registration. You should use the Voice VLAN interface for this. In this example, the IP Address is 10.0.201.1 for the VLAN 201 interface.

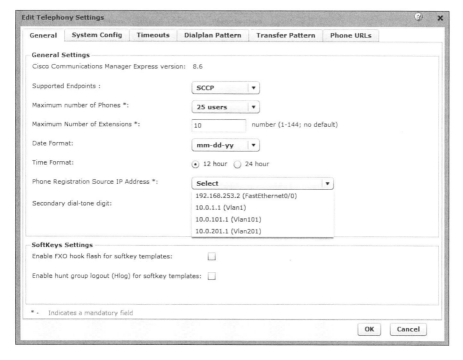

Figure 3-18   Choose the Phone Registration Source IP Address—In This Example, Use 10.0.201.1 (Vlan201)

8. The last field in the General Settings section is the Secondary dial-tone digit field. You can use a secondary dial-tone digit to access the PSTN or for long distance calling. For example, the number 9 is the most commonly used secondary dial-tone digit to access the PSTN for external calling (or to reach an outside line), as shown in Figure 3-19. There are other scenarios in which this may benefit you as well, such as dialing 8 for long distance calling or making an international call. When you select the text box, you can type in a number of your choice.

9. SoftKeys Settings — Enable FXO hook flash for softkey templates (Figure 3-20) is one of two options in the Softkeys Settings section on the General tab. If you use SCCP or SCCP and SIP as the endpoint configuration, you have the ability to enable hook flash, which is used for three-way calling and call-waiting within the PSTN.

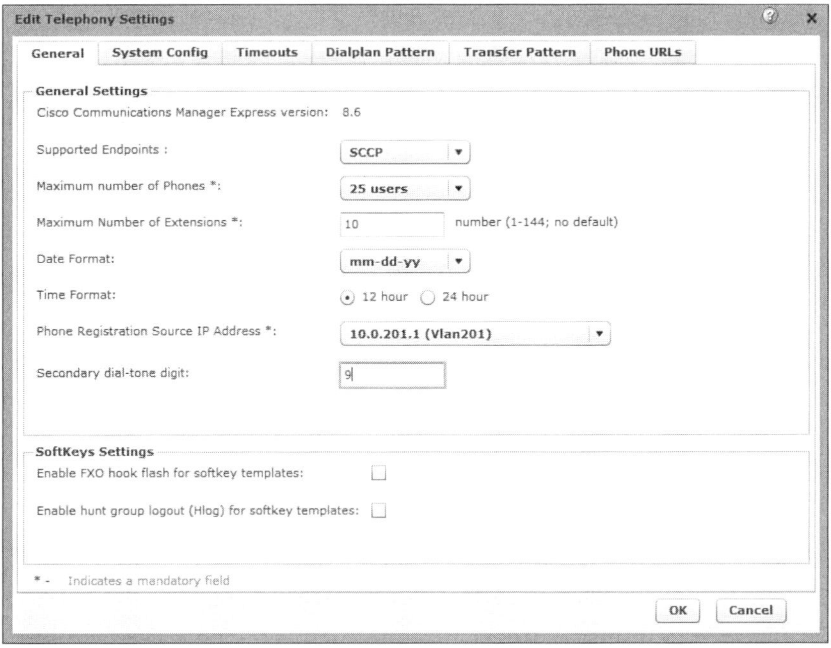

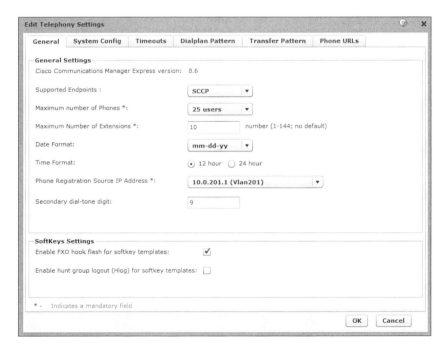

Figure 3-19   Secondary Dial-Tone Digit Field

Figure 3-20   Enable FXO Hook Flash for Softkey Templates

10. Enable hunt group logout (Hlog) for softkey templates is the second of the two options in the Softkeys Settings section of the General tab. As with the FXO hook flash, this feature is available if you use SCCP or SCCP and SIP as the endpoint configuration. With this feature, you have the ability to enable handling of DND (Do-Not-Disturb) separately. This is a more advanced feature than what is covered in the CCNA Voice certification, so leave this feature unchecked.

System Config Tab

1. On the second tab labeled System Config, there are administrative features that you can customize, as shown in Figure 3-21.

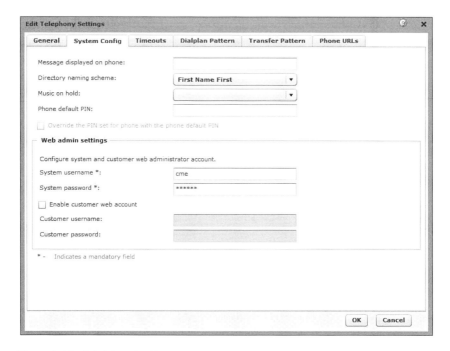

Figure 3-21 Administrative Features

2. Within the first field (Figure 3-22), you may specify a message to be displayed on the phone.

3. Within the Directory naming schema, you can choose from two options in the drop-down menu: First Name First or Last Name First.

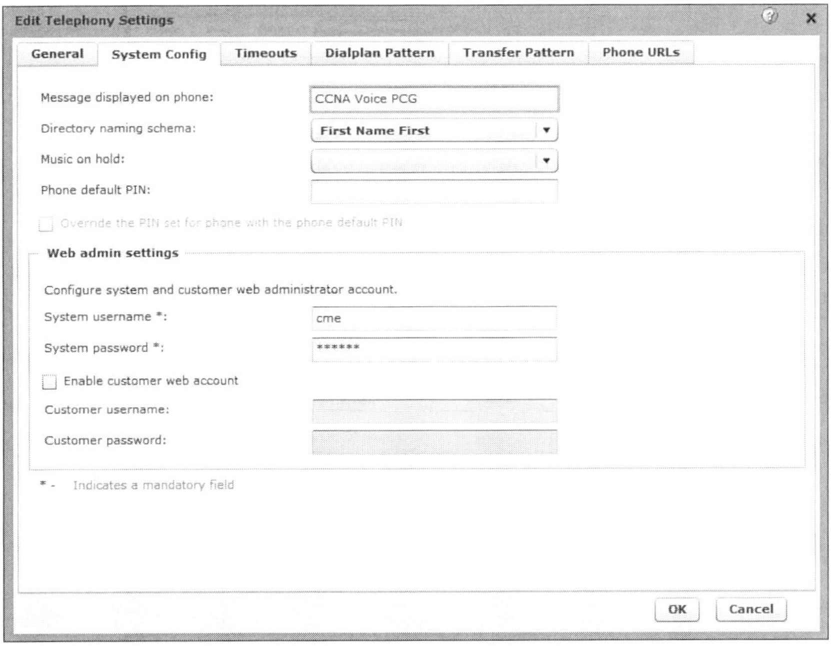

Figure 3-22   Message Displayed on Phone Field

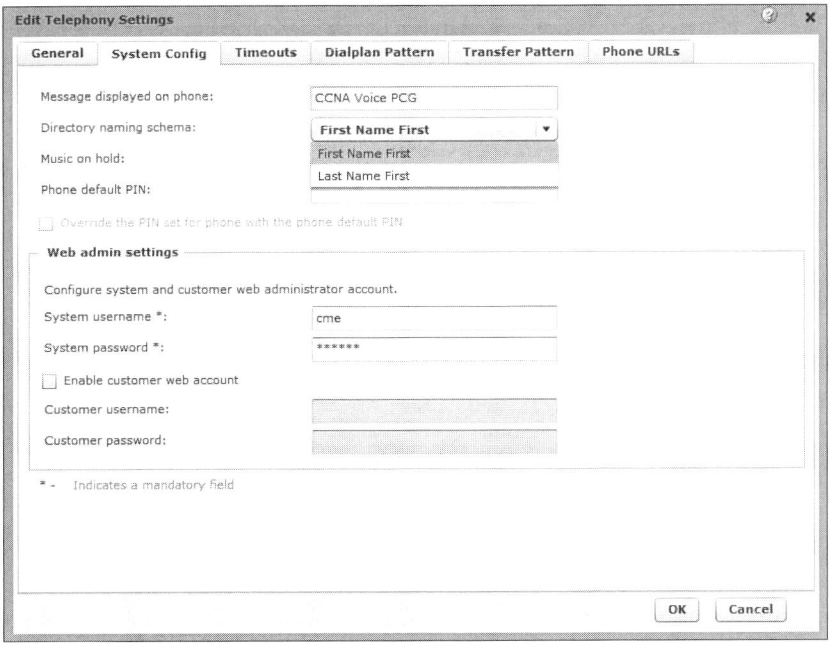

Figure 3-23   Directory Naming Schema Field

4. When you click the drop-down menu for Music on hold field (Figure 3-24), there are two different types of files that can populate the drop-down menu: .au and .wav. These files must be present in the router's flash memory before they appear in this drop-down menu.

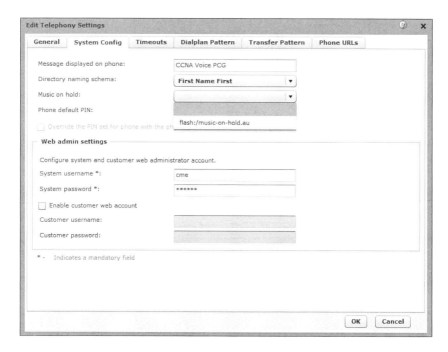

Figure 3-24 Music on Hold Field

5. In the Phone default PIN field (Figure 3-25), you have the option to configure a PIN. There is a check box to override the PIN set for the phone with the Phone Default PIN. It is a good idea to check this box when using a PIN. This can help with the overall management and administration of the phones.

Web Admin Settings

6. There is one required username and password to configure within the Web admin settings section on the System Config tab. This mandatory field is the System username. This example uses cme (refer to Figure 3-25); however, the most typical username used is admin or administrator. You may use any username and password combination you deem fit for your organization.

7. There is also one optional username and password to configure within the Web admin settings section on the System Config tab. This optional username is used for the Customer Web Account. For this example, use customer (Figure 3-26). Again, you may use any username and password combination you deem fit for your organization.

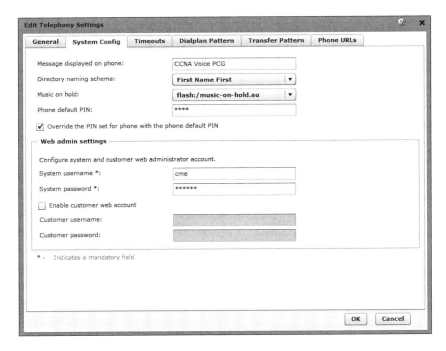

Figure 3-25   Phone Default PIN Field

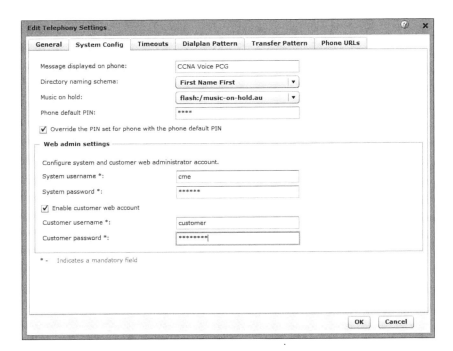

Figure 3-26   Web Admin Settings

When you are satisfied with these parameters, you can move onto the third tab from the left: the Timeouts tab.

Timeouts Tab

There are three timeout values to configure on the Timeouts tab:

- Interval Between Subsequent Digits Entered
- Wait Duration After Busy Tone
- Duration of Phone Ring Without Answer

NOTE It is typical to keep the defaults; however, there are some instances in which you may want to change these timeouts. This is truly dependent upon each organization's preference or based upon the business scenario. The default values are shown in Figure 3-27.

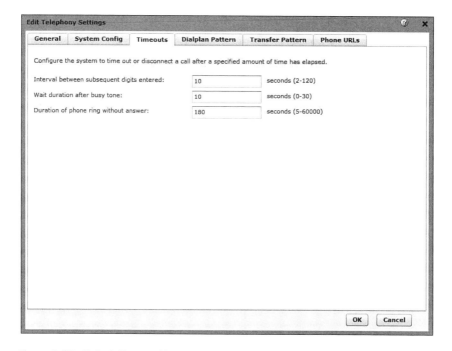

Figure 3-27   Default Timeout Values

Dialplan Pattern Tab

1. When using the Dialplan Pattern tab (see Figure 3-28), you can create multiple dialplan patterns by entering three required pieces of information and one optional piece of information. The Dialplan Pattern Information includes

- Pattern Tag

- Pattern

- Extension Length for the Caller ID

- Extension Number Leading Digit Pattern

■ E.164 Register (check box)

After you enter the appropriate information, click the **Add** button.

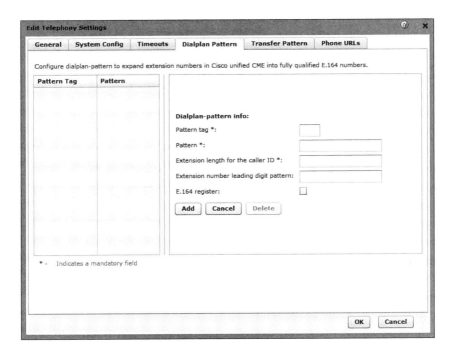

Figure 3-28   Dialplan Pattern Configuration Page

Figure 3-29 shows a sample configuration in which the first numbers in the dial-plan begin with 200.

After you click **OK**, the following screen appears (Figure 3-30) with the dialplan configured.

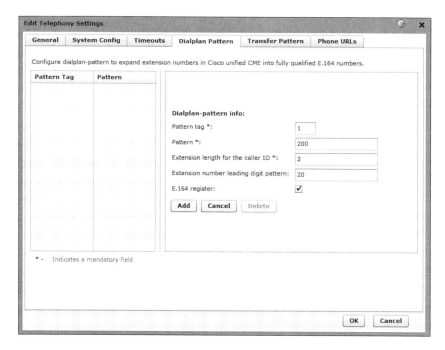

Figure 3-29   Dialplan Pattern Sample Configuration

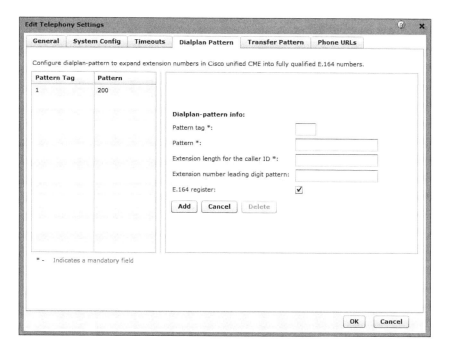

Figure 3-30   Dialplan Configured

You also can update (modify) or delete for the dialplan pattern you have previously created (Figure 3-31). If you would like to modify the dialplan pattern, simply
click the Pattern in the left pattern tag panel. After you have made your modifications, click the **Update** button to save the modification.

NOTE   You may not change the pattern tag. You must delete the pattern and then re-
create it with a different pattern tag.

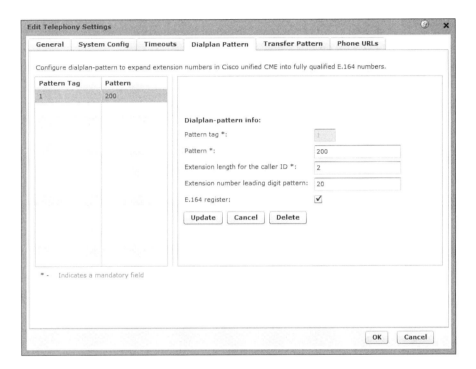

Figure 3-31   Modifying or Deleting Dialplan Patterns

2. If you need to delete a dialplan pattern for any reason, click the Pattern in the left
    pattern tag panel, and click the **Delete** button in the right configuration panel.

Transfer Pattern Tab

1. The next tab is the Transfer Pattern tab (Figure 3-32). Use this when you want to
    transfer a call from a Cisco IP Phone to a non-Cisco IP Phone.

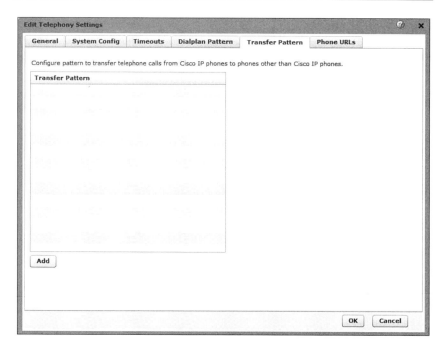

Figure 3-32   Transfer Pattern Tab

2. To configure a pattern, click the **Add** button on the bottom-left side of the window. A blue highlighted line appears, as shown in Figure 3-33.

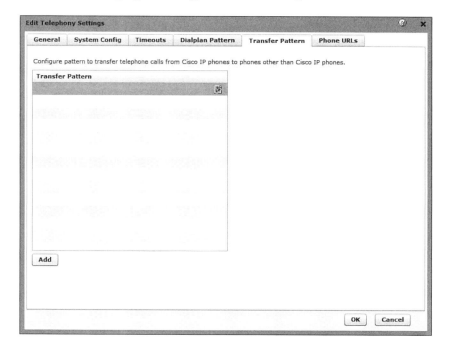

Figure 3-33   Transfer Pattern

3. Click the left side of the blue highlighted line and type in the pattern, as shown in Figure 3-34.

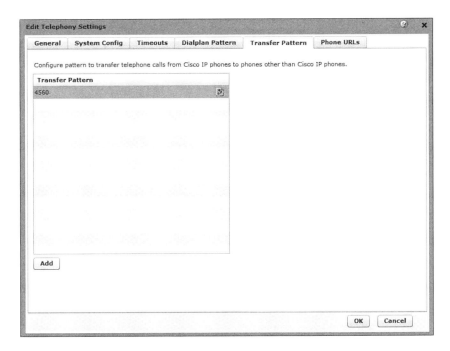

Figure 3-34 Phone Transfer Patterns

4. To delete a pattern, click the pattern you want to delete, and press **Delete**. In the current version of CCP, there is a slight bug that does not display the Delete button appropriately. The Delete button is the broken image in the middle of the page. (This should be resolved in a future release.)

Phone URLs Tab

1. On the Phone URLs tab, you can input customized URLs for the parameters shown in Figure 3-35.

2. After you complete all fields you want to complete at this time, click **OK**.

3. You receive the message shown in Figure 3-36, which states the phones need to be reset for the configuration changes you've made to take effect. You may either choose to reset the phones at this time or a later time.

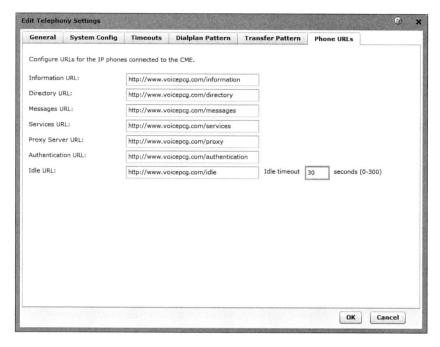

Figure 3-35   Customized URLs for IP Phones in CME

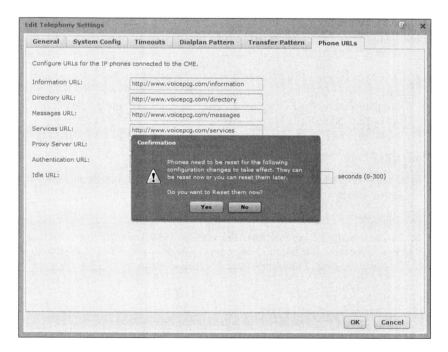

Figure 3-36   Confirmation to Reset Devices

4. Whether you choose to reset the phones now or later, another screen appears with the configuration script that was created for you by editing the telephony settings (Figure 3-37).

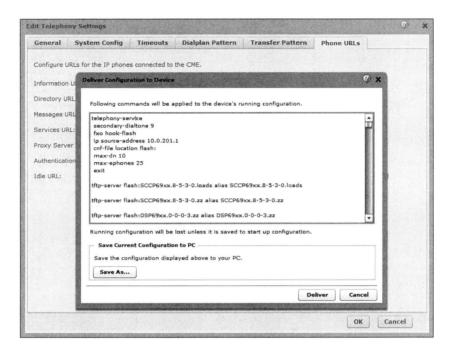

Figure 3-37 Configuration Script Created by Editing the Telephony Settings

At this point you may click the **Deliver** button. The full configuration script that was generated is here for your preview:

```
telephony-service
 secondary-dialtone 9
 fxo hook-flash
 ip source-address 10.0.201.1
 cnf-file location flash:
 max-dn 10
 max-ephones 25
 exit

tftp-server flash:SCCP69xx.8-5-3-0.loads alias SCCP69xx.8-5-3-0.loads

tftp-server flash:SCCP69xx.8-5-3-0.zz alias SCCP69xx.8-5-3-0.zz

tftp-server flash:DSP69xx.0-0-0-3.zz alias DSP69xx.0-0-0-3.zz
```

```
tftp-server flash:BOOT69xx.0-0-0-14.zz alias BOOT69xx.0-0-0-14.zz

tftp-server flash:SCCP11.8-5-3S.loads alias SCCP11.8-5-3S.loads

tftp-server flash:apps11.8-5-3TH1-6.sbn alias apps11.8-5-3TH1-6.sbn

tftp-server flash:cnu11.8-5-3TH1-6.sbn alias cnu11.8-5-3TH1-6.sbn

tftp-server flash:cvm11sccp.8-5-3TH1-6.sbn alias cvm11sccp.
  8-5-3TH1-6.sbn

tftp-server flash:dsp11.8-5-3TH1-6.sbn alias dsp11.8-5-3TH1-6.sbn

tftp-server flash:jar11sccp.8-5-3TH1-6.sbn alias jar11sccp.
  8-5-3TH1-6.sbn

tftp-server flash:term06.default.loads alias term06.default.loads

tftp-server flash:term11.default.loads alias term11.default.loads

tftp-server flash:B015-1-0-3.SBN alias B015-1-0-3.SBN

tftp-server flash:B016-1-0-3.SBN alias B016-1-0-3.SBN

tftp-server flash:CP7921G-1.3.3.LOADS alias CP7921G-1.3.3.LOADS

tftp-server flash:APPS-1.3.3.SBN alias APPS-1.3.3.SBN

tftp-server flash:GUI-1.3.3.SBN alias GUI-1.3.3.SBN

tftp-server flash:MISC-1.3.3.SBN alias MISC-1.3.3.SBN

tftp-server flash:SYS-1.3.3.SBN alias SYS-1.3.3.SBN

tftp-server flash:TNUX-1.3.3.SBN alias TNUX-1.3.3.SBN

tftp-server flash:WLAN-1.3.3.SBN alias WLAN-1.3.3.SBN

tftp-server flash:SCCP31.8-5-3S.loads alias SCCP31.8-5-3S.loads

tftp-server flash:apps31.8-5-3TH1-6.sbn alias apps31.8-5-3TH1-6.sbn

tftp-server flash:cnu31.8-5-3TH1-6.sbn alias cnu31.8-5-3TH1-6.sbn
```

```
tftp-server flash:cvm31sccp.8-5-3TH1-6.sbn alias cvm31sccp.
  8-5-3TH1-6.sbn

          .
tftp-server flash:dsp31.8-5-3TH1-6.sbn alias dsp31.8-5-3TH1-6.sbn

tftp-server flash:jar31sccp.8-5-3TH1-6.sbn alias jar31sccp.
  8-5-3TH1-6.sbn

tftp-server flash:term31.default.loads alias term31.default.loads

tftp-server flash:apps37sccp.1-3-4-0.bin alias apps37sccp.1-3-4-0.bin

tftp-server flash:SCCP41.8-5-3S.loads alias SCCP41.8-5-3S.loads

tftp-server flash:apps41.8-5-3TH1-6.sbn alias apps41.8-5-3TH1-6.sbn

tftp-server flash:cnu41.8-5-3TH1-6.sbn alias cnu41.8-5-3TH1-6.sbn

tftp-server flash:cvm41sccp.8-5-3TH1-6.sbn alias cvm41sccp.8-5-3TH1-6.
  sbn

tftp-server flash:dsp41.8-5-3TH1-6.sbn alias dsp41.8-5-3TH1-6.sbn

tftp-server flash:jar41sccp.8-5-3TH1-6.sbn alias jar41sccp.
  8-5-3TH1-6.sbn

tftp-server flash:term41.default.loads alias term41.default.loads

tftp-server flash:term61.default.loads alias term61.default.loads

tftp-server flash:SCCP42.8-5-3S.loads alias SCCP42.8-5-3S.loads

tftp-server flash:apps42.8-5-3TH1-6.sbn alias apps42.8-5-3TH1-6.sbn

tftp-server flash:cnu42.8-5-3TH1-6.sbn alias cnu42.8-5-3TH1-6.sbn

tftp-server flash:cvm42sccp.8-5-3TH1-6.sbn alias cvm42sccp.
  8-5-3TH1-6.sbn

tftp-server flash:dsp42.8-5-3TH1-6.sbn alias dsp42.8-5-3TH1-6.sbn

tftp-server flash:jar42sccp.8-5-3TH1-6.sbn alias jar42sccp.
  8-5-3TH1-6.sbn

tftp-server flash:term42.default.loads alias term42.default.loads
```

```
tftp-server flash:term62.default.loads alias term62.default.loads

tftp-server flash:SCCP45.8-5-3S.loads alias SCCP45.8-5-3S.loads

tftp-server flash:apps45.8-5-3TH1-6.sbn alias apps45.8-5-3TH1-6.sbn

tftp-server flash:cnu45.8-5-3TH1-6.sbn alias cnu45.8-5-3TH1-6.sbn

tftp-server flash:cvm45sccp.8-5-3TH1-6.sbn alias cvm45sccp.
  8-5-3TH1-6.sbn

tftp-server flash:dsp45.8-5-3TH1-6.sbn alias dsp45.8-5-3TH1-6.sbn

tftp-server flash:jar45sccp.8-5-3TH1-6.sbn alias jar45sccp.
  8-5-3TH1-6.sbn

tftp-server flash:term45.default.loads alias term45.default.loads

tftp-server flash:term65.default.loads alias term65.default.loads

tftp-server flash:SCCP75.8-5-3S.loads alias SCCP75.8-5-3S.loads

tftp-server flash:apps75.8-5-3TH1-6.sbn alias apps75.8-5-3TH1-6.sbn

tftp-server flash:cnu75.8-5-3TH1-6.sbn alias cnu75.8-5-3TH1-6.sbn

tftp-server flash:cvm75sccp.8-5-3TH1-6.sbn alias cvm75sccp.
  8-5-3TH1-6.sbn

tftp-server flash:dsp75.8-5-3TH1-6.sbn alias dsp75.8-5-3TH1-6.sbn

tftp-server flash:jar75sccp.8-5-3TH1-6.sbn alias jar75sccp.
  8-5-3TH1-6.sbn

tftp-server flash:term75.default.loads alias term75.default.loads

tftp-server flash:SCCP70.8-5-3S.loads alias SCCP70.8-5-3S.loads

tftp-server flash:apps70.8-5-3TH1-6.sbn alias apps70.8-5-3TH1-6.sbn

tftp-server flash:cnu70.8-5-3TH1-6.sbn alias cnu70.8-5-3TH1-6.sbn

tftp-server flash:cvm70sccp.8-5-3TH1-6.sbn alias cvm70sccp.
  8-5-3TH1-6.sbn
```

```
tftp-server flash:dsp70.8-5-3TH1-6.sbn alias dsp70.8-5-3TH1-6.sbn

tftp-server flash:jar70sccp.8-5-3TH1-6.sbn alias jar70sccp.
  8-5-3TH1-6.sbn

tftp-server flash:term70.default.loads alias term70.default.loads

tftp-server flash:term71.default.loads alias term71.default.loads

telephony-service
 load 6921 SCCP69xx.8-5-3-0.loads
 create cnf-files
 exit

telephony-service
 load 6941 SCCP69xx.8-5-3-0.loads
 create cnf-files
 exit

telephony-service
 load 6961 SCCP69xx.8-5-3-0.loads
 create cnf-files
 exit

telephony-service
 load 7906 SCCP11.8-5-3S.loads
 create cnf-files
 exit

telephony-service
 load 7911 SCCP11.8-5-3S.loads
 create cnf-files
 exit

telephony-service
 load 7915-12 B015-1-0-3.SBN
 create cnf-files
 exit

telephony-service
 load 7915-24 B015-1-0-3.SBN
 create cnf-files
 exit
```

```
telephony-service
 load 7916-12 B016-1-0-3.SBN
 create cnf-files
 exit

telephony-service
 load 7916-24 B016-1-0-3.SBN
 create cnf-files
 exit

telephony-service
 load 7921 CP7921G-1.3.3.LOADS
 create cnf-files
 exit

telephony-service
 load 7931 SCCP31.8-5-3S.loads
 create cnf-files
 exit

telephony-service
 load 7937 apps37sccp.1-3-4-0.bin
 create cnf-files
 exit

telephony-service
 load 7941 SCCP41.8-5-3S.loads
 create cnf-files
 exit

telephony-service
 load 7961 SCCP41.8-5-3S.loads
 create cnf-files
 exit

telephony-service
 load 7941GE SCCP41.8-5-3S.loads
 create cnf-files
 exit

telephony-service
 load 7961GE SCCP41.8-5-3S.loads
 create cnf-files
 exit
```

```
telephony-service
 load 7942 SCCP42.8-5-3S.loads
 create cnf-files
 exit

telephony-service
 load 7962 SCCP42.8-5-3S.loads
 create cnf-files
 exit

telephony-service
 load 7945 SCCP45.8-5-3S.loads
 create cnf-files
 exit

telephony-service
 load 7965 SCCP45.8-5-3S.loads
 create cnf-files
 exit

telephony-service
 load 7975 SCCP75.8-5-3S.loads
 create cnf-files
 exit

telephony-service
 load 7970 SCCP70.8-5-3S.loads
 create cnf-files
 exit

telephony-service
 load 7971 SCCP70.8-5-3S.loads
 create cnf-files
 exit

telephony-service
 create cnf-files
 reset all
 exit

telephony-service
 url idle http://www.voicepcg.com/idle idle-timeout 30
 url services http://www.voicepcg.com/services
```

```
url proxy-server http://www.voicepcg.com/proxy
url messages http://www.voicepcg.com/messages
url information http://www.voicepcg.com/information
url directories http://www.voicepcg.com/directory
url authentication http://www.voicepcg.com/authentication
web admin customer name customer secret 0 customer
dialplan-pattern 1 200 extension-length 2 extension-pattern 20
moh flash:/music-on-hold.au
system message CCNA Voice PCG
pin 1234 override
create cnf-files
reset all
exit
```

5. You have successfully configured the preliminary parameters for telephony on this router. You are now ready to begin configuring users, phones, and other parameters necessary for a full voice system. You can see the parameters you configured from the telephony settings page in Figure 3-38.

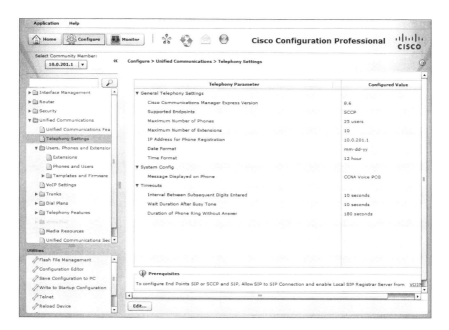

Figure 3-38   Verifying Telephony Settings Configuration

CHAPTER 4

Cisco Unified CME Features

This chapter provides information and commands concerning the following topics:

- Creating Extensions
- Modifying Extensions
- Deleting Extensions
- Cloning Extensions
- Creating Phones and Users
- Modifying Phones and Users
- Deleting Phones and Users
- Other Telephony Features

Creating Extensions

This section refers to the network topology shown in Figure 4-1 and provides details about the options you have when creating extensions within CUCME using the CCP.

1. From the left navigation panel within the CCP, click **Extensions**.

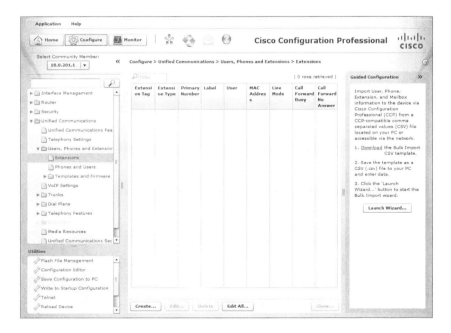

Figure 4-1   Creating Extensions

NOTE   If you receive an error, such as the one shown in Figure 4-2, you must enable
the telephony service by going to Telephony Settings in the left navigation panel (see
Chapter 3, "Cisco Unified Communications Manager Express," for more details).

Figure 4-2   Informational Warning

2.   There are a few different ways to create extensions. The first is to create ephone-
     DNs within the CLI. The second is to import user, phone, extension, and mailbox
     information using a comma-separated value (CSV) file. The third is to create each
     user, phone, and extension manually using the CCP. You guessed it; this is the
     way to proceed for now.

     Click the **Create** button on the lower-left side of the right configuration panel,
     and another dialog box appears (see Figure 4.3).

Figure 4-3   Create Extensions Dialog Box

3. On the left navigation panel, there are multiple items to configure. The first one is General. This is actually the only screen required to be configured and have some user intervention. On the right configuration panel, you see the General heading. Under the General heading are several parameters to configure. The first and fore-most field is the Primary number field. This field can simply be a four-digit exten-sion, as shown in Figure 4-4.

Figure 4-4   Create Extensions — General Tab — Primary Number

4. The next field is the Secondary number. This is an optional field; however, it is a useful one. One of the best options for this field is to enter the 10-digit phone number (Figure 4-5).

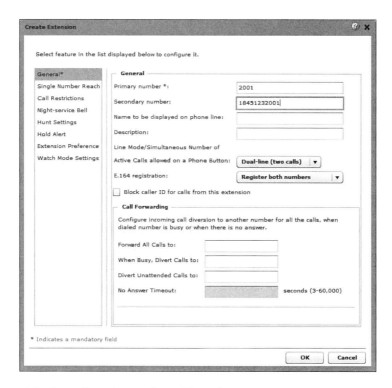

Figure 4-5   Create Extensions — General Tab—Secondary Number

5. Within the next field, Name To Be Displayed On Phone Line, enter the person's name, or if it is a reception area, you can simply put reception, lobby, or something else that pertains to the general area the phone resides in (Figure 4-6).

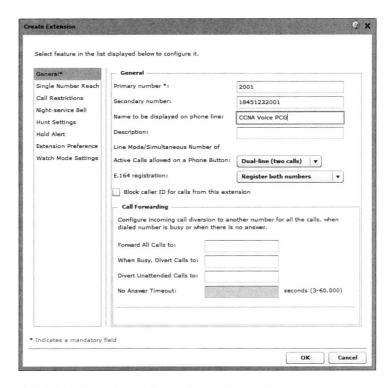

Figure 4-6   Create Extensions — General Tab — Display Name

6. You also have the choice to place a description within the phone. (The author typically places the location of the phone in the description field ([Figure 4-7].)

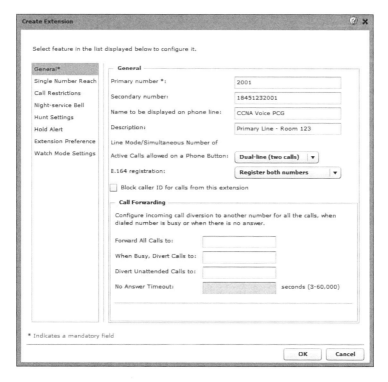

Figure 4-7   Create Extensions — General Tab — Description

7. In the next field, there is a drop-down menu for Line Mode/Simultaneous Number of Active Calls Allowed on a Phone Button (Figure 4-8). You have three options:

   - **Dual-line:** You can have two simultaneous calls; this is typical because you have the ability for call waiting and conference calling.

   - **Single-line:** You can make or receive only one call at a time; this is great for a breakroom area or waiting room.

   - **Octo-line:** You can have eight simultaneous calls; this would be useful for a receptionist.

8. On the E.164 registration drop-down menu, you have four options (Figure 4-9):

   - **Register Both Numbers:** This is typical if using a primary and secondary number; however, this is decided on a per-case basis.

   - **Do Not Register Any Number**

   - **Register Secondary Number**

   - **Register Primary Number**

     Where each phone is located determines which type of registration will be required.

Figure 4-8 How Many Active Calls Are Permitted on the Phone at One Time?

Figure 4-9 E.164 Registration

9. There is a check box to Block Caller ID for Calls from This Extension as well (Figure 4-10). This can be beneficial depending upon the role the individual plays within an organization.

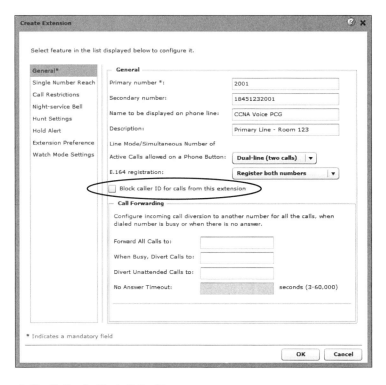

Figure 4-10   Option to Block Caller ID

10. The next section is Call Forwarding. In this section, you have four options configured on a per-case basis:

   ▪ **Forward All Calls to**

   ▪ **When Busy, Divert Calls to**

   ▪ **Divert Unattended Calls to**

   ▪ **No Answer Timeout:** This feature is not supported when SIP phones fall back to SRST mode within the CUCME.

11. On the left navigation panel within the Create Extensions dialog box, click **Single Number Reach** (Figure 4-11). This is a great feature that enables users to have the ultimate flexibility to answer incoming calls on their normal IP Phone, on their mobile phone, or on a softphone that resides in software on their desktop or laptop. There are four options within this page when the Enable SNR for This Extension check box is checked:

■ **Remote Number:** This is another phone number that can be called.

■ **Ring Remote Number After:** This is a value in seconds where the remote number will be called.

■ **Timeout:** This is a value in seconds where the incoming call will timeout and be forwarded.

■ **Forward Unanswered Calls to:** This is a phone number that is called if the incoming call is not answered.

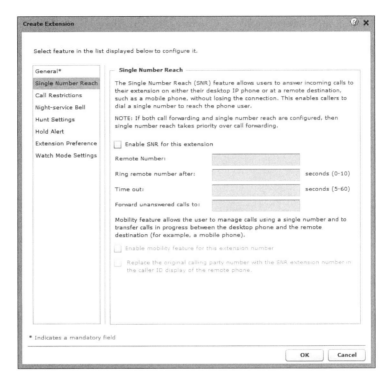

Figure 4-11   Single Number Reach

12. On the left navigation panel within the Create Extensions dialog box, click **Call Restrictions** (Figure 4-12). This is where you can apply permissions to this extension.

NOTE   You must first create the permissions within the dial plan section of CCP.

Figure 4-12   Call Restrictions

13. On the left navigation panel within the Create Extensions dialog box, click **Night-Service Bell** (Figure 4-13). This feature is great if you do not have 24/7/365 coverage for an onsite help desk.

14. On the left navigation panel within the Create Extensions dialog box, click **Hunt Settings** (Figure 4-14). Use Hunt settings when an incoming call receives a busy signal or a call is not answered. The incoming call can be rolled over to another extension when the first number dialed is either busy or not answered on a certain number of rings.

Figure 4-13   Night-Service Bell

Figure 4-14   Hunt Settings

15. On the left navigation panel within the Create Extensions dialog box, click **Hold Alert** (Figure 4-15). Use this feature to configure an audible notification for calls on hold.

    You can change when the alert (or notification) is activated using one of four options:

    - **Idle or Busy**
    - **Idle**
    - **Shared**
    - **Shared-Idle**

Figure 4-15 Hold Alert Options

    You can also repeat the alert at a set interval.

16. On the left navigation panel within the Create Extensions dialog box, click **Extension Preference** (Figure 4-16). This enables you to specify the order of preference for which line is selected when you have multiple lines configured with the same extension number.

17. On the left navigation panel within the Create Extensions dialog box, click **Watch Mode Settings** (Figure 4-17). This enables the status of a particular extension to be watched so that you can see whether the phone line is busy or idle.

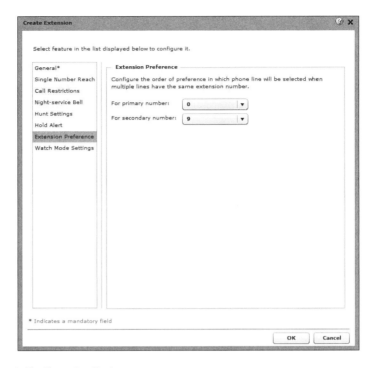

Figure 4-16 Extension Preference

Figure 4-17 Watch Mode Settings

18. When you finish configuring all the options you want to set at this time, click the **OK** button at the bottom of the dialog box. Another dialog box appears asking you to verify the CLI commands that have been generated using CCP that will be sent to the router (Figure 4-18).

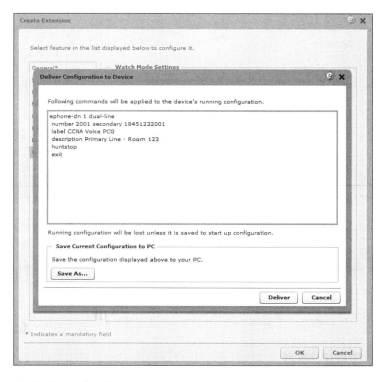

Figure 4-18   Deliver Configuration to Device

19. Click **Deliver** if you are satisfied with the syntax generated.

20. You should now see the screen shown in Figure 4-19 on the Configuration tab of the CCP (after the configuration has been delivered to the router and has completed successfully).

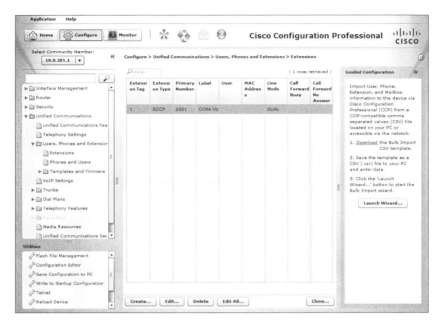

Figure 4-19   You Now Have a Successful Extension Created

Modifying Extensions

This section provides details about modifying extensions within CUCME using the CCP.

1. On the left navigation panel within the CCP, click **Extensions**.

2. You have two options for modifying/editing extensions within the CCP:

   ▪ **Edit**

   ▪ **Edit All**

3. If you click **Edit**, the extensive Edit Extensions dialog box appears (Figure 4-20). You can modify all the options discussed about creating an extension with the same tabs as referenced previously. After you make the necessary changes, click **OK**.

4. If you click **Edit All**, a different window appears (Figure 4-21). This window enables you to modify each field within a tabular format such as a spreadsheet. You may add or delete extensions from this dialog box as well.

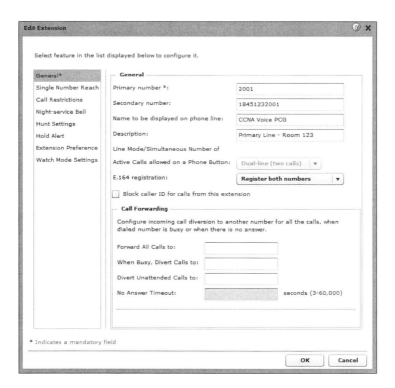

Figure 4-20   Edit Extensions

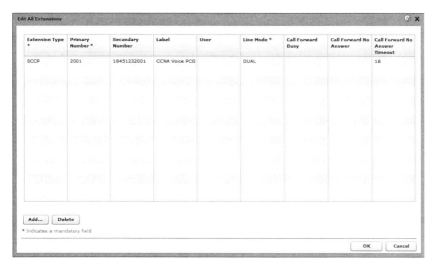

Figure 4-21   Edit All Extensions Screen

Deleting Extensions

This section provides details about deleting extensions within CUCME using the CCP.

1. On the left navigation panel within the CCP, click **Extensions**.

2. You have two options for deleting extensions within the CCP:

   ■ Use the **Delete** button at the bottom of the Extensions configuration panel. Keep in mind that you must click **Yes** to confirm this deletion (Figure 4-22).

Figure 4-22 Deleting an Extension Confirmation Screen

   ■ Use the **Delete** button after clicking the **Edit All** button at the bottom of the Extensions configuration panel.

3. After you make the necessary deletions, click **OK**.

NOTE You may need to select the extensions you want to edit prior to clicking **Edit All**. Otherwise, you may see only one extension in the Edit All Extensions dialog box. You should also be aware that this method will NOT ask you to confirm this deletion; however, the extension will not be deleted until you click **OK**, as shown in Figure 4-23.

Figure 4-23 Make Sure You Click OK to Complete the Process

4. Don't forget to save your configuration to **nvram** (**startup-config**) after you make any changes. Click **Write to Startup Configuration** on the bottom-left navigation panel under Utilities; then click **Confirm** on the right configuration panel (Figure 4-24).

Figure 4-24   Saving Your Configuration

Cloning Extensions

This section provides details about cloning extensions within CUCME using the CCP to help speed up administration/creation of additional extensions.

1. On the left navigation panel within the CCP, click **Extensions**.

2. Highlight the extension you want to clone, and click **Clone** (Figure 4-25).

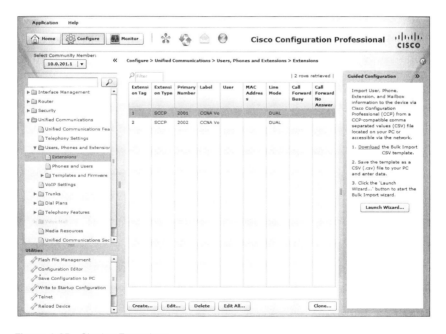

Figure 4-25   Cloning Extensions

3. The Create Extension dialog box appears with all the same parameters completed from the extension you are cloning. Change the primary number and any other information such as secondary number, name, description, and so on and click **OK** (Figure 4-26). You now have an additional extension with all the same parameters configured as the extension you are cloning from.

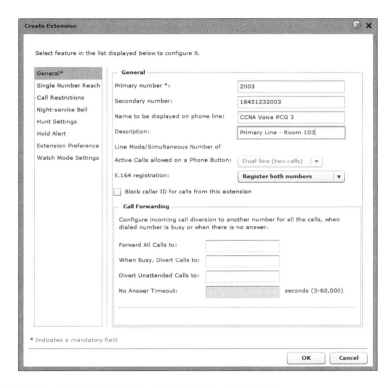

Figure 4-26 Changing Information While Cloning Extensions

Creating Phones and Users

This section provides details about creating phones and users within CUCME using the CCP.

1. On the left navigation panel within the CCP, click the **Users, Phones and Extensions** folder; then click **Phones and Users** (Figure 4-27).

2. On the right pane, click **Create**. The Create Phone/User dialog box appears (Figure 4-28).

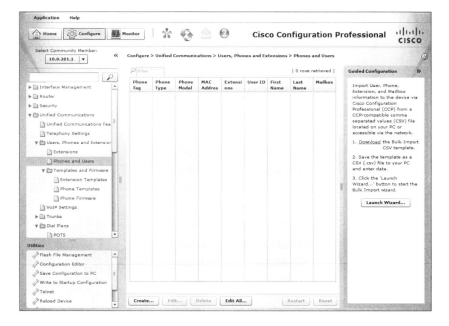

Figure 4-27   Phones and Users

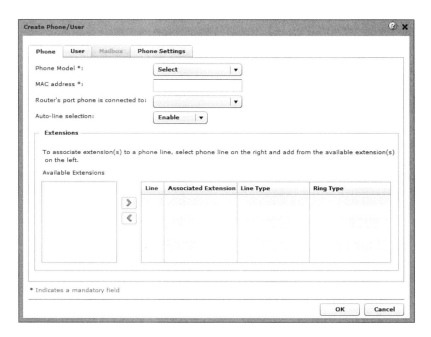

Figure 4-28   Phone Tab Within Creating Phones/Users

3. On the Phone tab, begin by selecting the phone model you use from the drop-down menu (Figure 4-29).

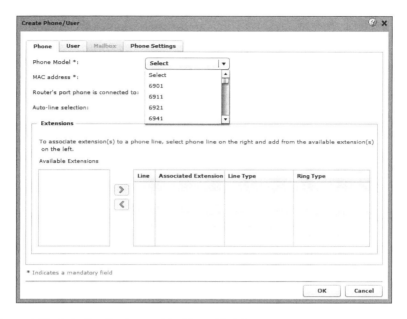

Figure 4-29 Selecting the Appropriate Phone Model

NOTE There are more phone choices than what is displayed in Figure 4-29.

4. After you select a phone model, the available extensions section on the bottom auto-
    matically populates if you have previously configured extensions (Figure 4-30).

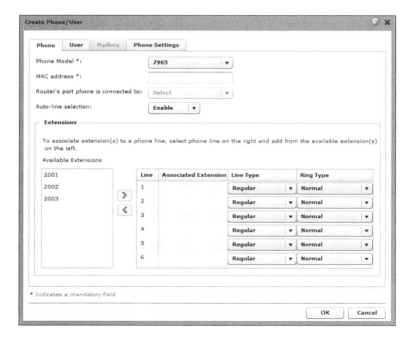

Figure 4-30 Available Extensions for Phone Configuration

5. The next field you are required to complete is the MAC address field of the phone (Figure 4-31). You can find this on the bottom of the Cisco IP Phone.

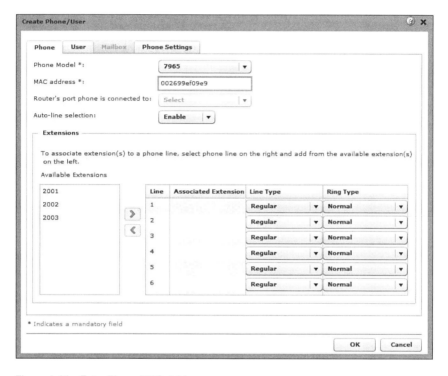

Figure 4-31 Enter Phone MAC Address

In this scenario there is an option that is grayed out named Router's Port Phone Is Connected To. This option is used to specify if there is a device connected to the IP Phone built-in switch.

6. In the Auto-line selection field (Figure 4-32), you have three options to choose from:
   - **Enable**
   - **Disable**
   - **Incoming**

7. If you have added extensions, there are available extensions that you may associate to a specific line on the phone (Figure 4-33). The phone model you choose determines how many lines are available for you. The model phone the author uses is the Cisco 7965G, which has six lines. (This means there are six buttons on the top-right side of the phone.)

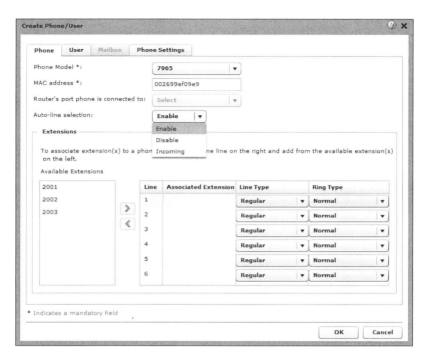

Figure 4-32 Auto-Line Selection

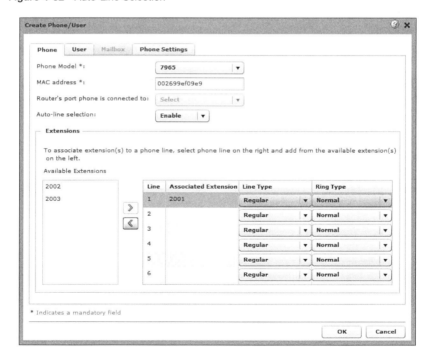

Figure 4-33 Adding an Extension to the Phone

8. On the Extensions section at the bottom of the Phone tab, you have two other options after you associate an extension to a specific line on the phone (Figure 4-34):

- **Line Type**

- **Ring Type:** On the Line Type drop-down menu, you have four options:

- **Regular:** One number is assigned to one phone.

- **Overlay:** These are numbers that share the same button on a phone.

- **Monitor:** One number is shared by two people. When one person is on a call, the other can see if the line is being used.

- **Call Waiting on Overlay:** This enables a person to know when another phone call is being received while also being on the phone.

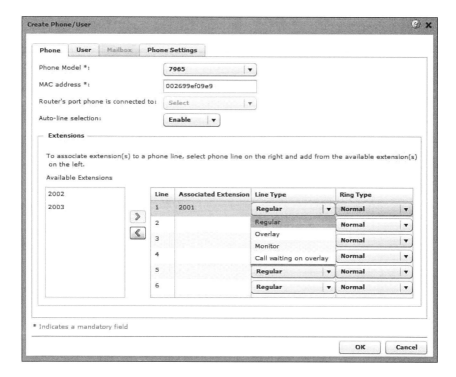

Figure 4-34 Line Type Options

On the Ring Type drop-down menu, you have four options (Figure 4-35):

- **Normal**

- **Feature:** This is a rather unique option where a triple-pulse cadence is heard on incoming calls.

- **Beep**

- **Silent**

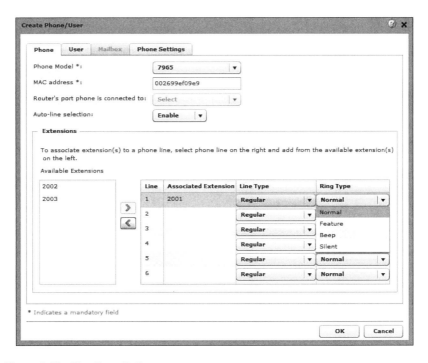

Figure 4-35   Ring Type Options

9. Click the User tab at the top, and type in a user ID for this phone (Figure 4-36). This is optional but useful!

Figure 4-36   User Creation

10. In the First Name field, type the first name; in the Last Name field, type the last name (Figure 4-37). You will not be permitted to have spaces, so the user John Edward Jones would either need to be John Jones or JohnEdward Jones.

Figure 4-37   User Creation Example

11. The next field is a drop-down menu for Password Generation (Figure 4-38). You have two options:

   ▪ **Use Blank Password**
   ▪ **Use Custom Password Below**

Figure 4-38   User Creation — Password Generation Options

If you choose **Use Blank Password**, the New Password and Confirm Password fields are grayed out (Figure 4-39).

Figure 4-39   Password Generation — Use Blank Password Option

If you choose **Use Custom Password Below**, you must enter a password in the New Password and the Confirm Password fields, and they must match (Figure 4-40).

Figure 4-40   Password Generation — Use Custom Password Below Option

12. The PIN Generation drop-down menu has two options (Figure 4-41):

- **Use Blank PIN**
- **Use Custom PIN Below**

Figure 4-41   PIN Generation Options

If you choose **Use Blank PIN**, the New PIN and Confirm PIN fields are grayed out, as shown in Figure 4-42.

Figure 4-42   PIN Generation — Use Blank PIN Option

If you choose **Use Custom PIN Below**, you must enter a PIN in the New PIN and the Confirm PIN fields, and they must match (Figure 4-43).

Figure 4-43   PIN Generation — Use Custom PIN Below Option

NOTE   At this point, the Mailbox tab will be grayed out because this is not set up yet.

13. Click the Phone Settings tab at the top. There are three sections that are all optional (Figure 4-44):

   ▪ **Night Service**

   ▪ **Enable Remote Worker**

   ▪ **Speed Dial**

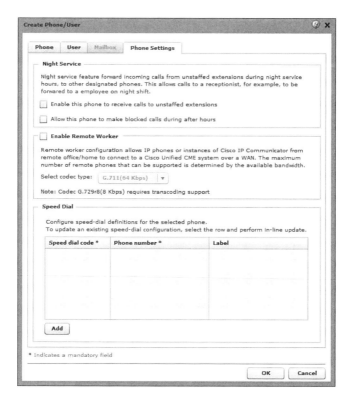

Figure 4-44   Phone Settings

If you select the **Enable Remote Worker** check box, you have the option to select the type of codec you would like to use from the drop-down menu (Figure 4-45).

If you add a speed dial setting, you can simply type in the Speed Dial code cell, Phone Number cell, and the Label cell (Figure 4-46).

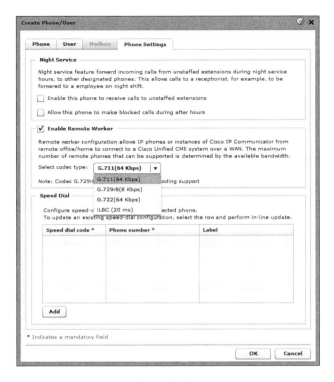

Figure 4-45 Enable Remote Worker Codec Options

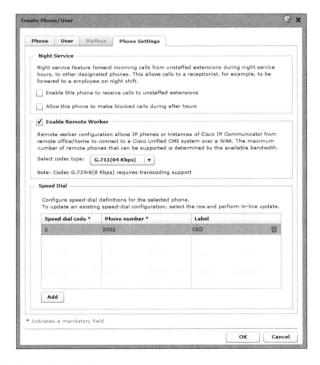

Figure 4-46 Speed Dial Settings

14. After you are satisfied with the settings for this phone and user, click **OK**. You are then prompted with the dialog box shown in Figure 4-47.

Figure 4-47 User Creation Confirmation/Reset Message

After you click **Yes** or **No**, you are prompted with another dialog box requesting permission to deliver the configuration to the device (the router in this case), as shown in Figure 4-48.

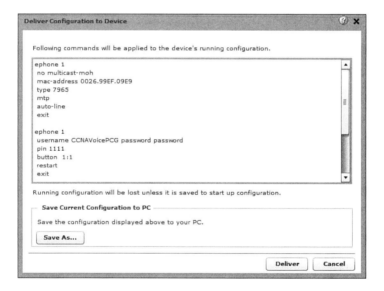

Figure 4-48 Deliver Configuration to the Router

The Cisco CLI IOS syntax that will be delivered to the router is

```
ephone 1
 no multicast-moh
 mac-address 0026.99EF.09E9
 type 7965
 mtp
 auto-line
 exit
```

```
ephone 1
  username CCNAVoicePCG password password
  pin 1111
  button  1:1
  restart
  exit
ephone-dn 1
  name CCNA VoicePCG
  exit

ephone 1
  speed-dial 2 2002 label "CEO"
  restart
  exit
```

After you click **Deliver**, the syntax is delivered to the router and added to the **running-config**. After the delivery of the configuration to the router is complete, the IP Phone resets (if you chose **Yes** to reset the IP Phone) and you see the screen shown in Figure 4-49 on the CCP within the Phones and Users configuration pane.

Figure 4-49 Phone and Users Configuration Screen

Modifying Phones and Users

This section provides details about modifying phones and users within CUCME using the CCP.

1. On the left navigation panel within the CCP, click **Phones and Users** within the **Users, Phones and Extensions** folder.

2. You have two options for modifying/editing extensions within the CCP:

   ▪ **Edit**

   ▪ **Edit All**

3. Before the **Edit** option is available for you to click, you must click one of the endpoints to modify. This row is now highlighted (Figure 4-50). If you click **Edit**, the extensive Edit Phone/User dialog box appears. You can modify all the options discussed with the same tabs as referenced with two exceptions: the Phone Model and the MAC Address. After you make the necessary changes, click **OK**.

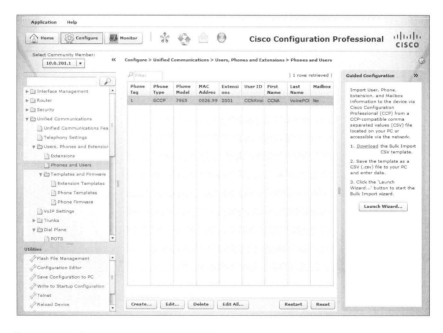

Figure 4-50 Phone and User Modification

4. If you click **Edit All**, a different window appears. This window enables you to modify each field within a tabular format such as a spreadsheet, as shown in Figure 4-51. You may add or delete users and phones from this dialog box as well.

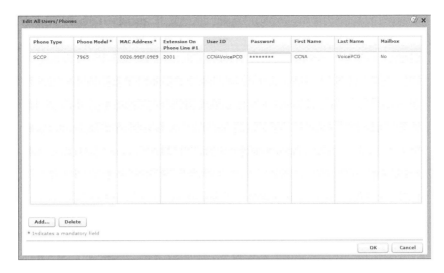

Figure 4-51 Edit All Users/Phones

Deleting Phones and Users

This section provides details about deleting phones and users within CUCME using the CCP.

1. On the left navigation panel within the CCP, click **Phones and Users** within the **Users, Phones and Extensions** folder.

2. You have two options for deleting phones and users within the CCP (Figure 4-52):

   ■ Using the **Delete** button at the bottom of the Extensions configuration panel. Note: This requires confirmation by clicking **Yes**.

   ■ Using the **Delete** button after clicking the **Edit All** button at the bottom of the Phones and Users configuration panel. Note: This method will NOT ask you for a confirmation; however, the item is not deleted until you click **OK** (Figure 4-53).

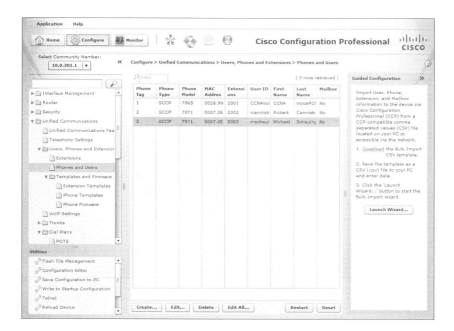

Figure 4-52 Deleting Users, Phones and Extensions

Figure 4-53 Deletions of Users/Phones

3. After you make the necessary deletions, click **OK**.

NOTE   You may need to select the phone and user you want to edit prior to clicking **Edit All**; otherwise, you may see only one extension in the Edit All Extensions dialog box. Figure 4-54 shows an example of selecting all the phones and users within the configuration panel.

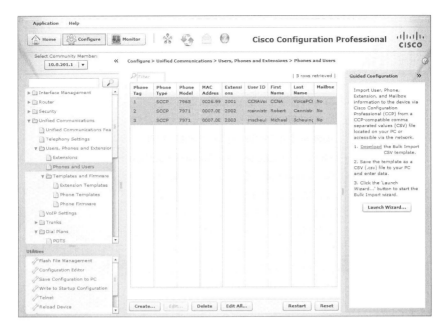

Figure 4-54   Phones and Users

Other Telephony Features

This section provides a brief overview of the other telephony features found within the CUCME. These features will be discussed in the CUCM chapters of this portable command guide. If you click the Telephony Features folder in the left navigation panel, you see a list of features that can be enabled in CUCME, as shown in Figure 4-55. Each feature depends on how the organization uses CUCME and is configured on a per case basis. The features include

- After-Hour Toolbar
- Auto Attendant
  - Basic Automatic Call Distribution
  - Prompts and Scripts
  - Call Conference
- Call Park
- Call Pickup Groups
- Directory Services
- Hunt Groups
- Intercom

■ Night Service Bell

■ Paging Numbers

■ Paging Groups

NOTE A subset of these features are covered in Chapter 6, "Cisco Unified Communications Manager (CUCM) Telephony and Mobility Features."

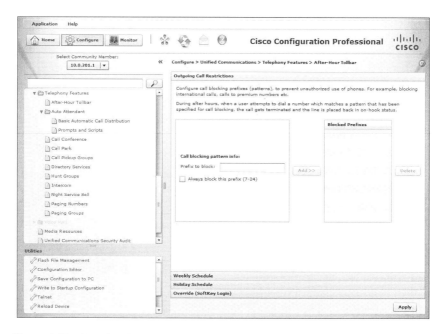

Figure 4-55 Outgoing Call Restrictions

CHAPTER 5

Cisco Unified Communications Manager (CUCM) Administration and Management

This chapter provides information and commands concerning the following topics:

- Cisco Unified Communications Manager Administration Interfaces
- Accessing the Management GUI and CLI Interfaces
- Changing CUCM Name to IP Address for DNS Independence
- Configuring a Unified CM Group
- Configuring a Phone NTP Reference
- Configuring a Date/Time Group
- Configuring Locations
- Configuring Device Pools
- Configuring a Partition
- Configuring a Calling Search Space
- Activating Services and Features
- Creating a Phone Button Template
- Creating a Softkey Template
- Creating a Common Phone Profile
- Creating an Application User with Administrative Rights
- Creating an Application User with Read-Only Rights
- Creating an End User Manually
- Adding Users via LDAP Synchronization
- Configuring LDAP Authentication for End Users
- Adding an IP Phone to CUCM Manually
- Adding a Directory Number (DN) to a Phone
- Adding Phones Using Auto-registration
- Adding End Users and Phones with the Bulk Administration Tool (BAT)
- Configuring an H.323 Gateway in CUCM
- Configuring a Route Pattern

Topology

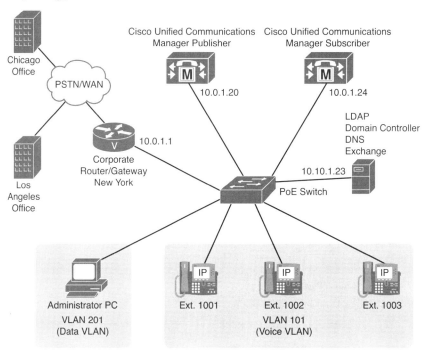

Figure 5-1   Cisco Unified Communications Manager Administration Topology

Cisco Unified Communications Manager Administration Interfaces

There are six administration interfaces for the Cisco Unified Communications Manager. Five interfaces are available via web-based GUI and one CLI is available via SSH. The author found it confusing to remember which login to use for a particular administration interface. To help you avoid the same confusion, Table 5-1 lists the name of the administration interface, the method to access the interface, and what username and password to use.

If you have only one Call Manager, all administration is performed on that single node. But if you have a cluster of two or more Call Managers, all administration should be performed on the Call Manager Publisher using its IP address, as shown in Table 5-1.

Table 5-1   Administration Interface Reference

Administration Interface	Access Method	Username/Password Combo
Cisco Unified Communications Manager Administration	https://<IPAddress>/ ccmadmin	Application Username/ Password

Administration Interface	Access Method	Username/Password Combo
Cisco Unified Service-ability	https://<IPAddress>/ccmservice	Application Username/Password
Cisco Unified OS Admin-istration	https://<IPAddress>/cmplatform	Platform Username/Password
Disaster Recovery System	https://<IPAddress>/drf	Platform Username/Password
Cisco Unified Reporting	https://<IPAddress>/cucreports	Application Username/Password
Command Line Interface	SSH to <IPAddress>	Platform Username/Password
NOTE There is a web interface for end users to configure their own device and mobility settings. Their End User account must belong to correct User Group for web page access. See "Creating an End User Manually" for more information. The End User web interface is not generally considered an Administration Interface; it's included here as an FYI.		
End User Web Pages	https://<IPAddress>/ccmuser	End UserID /Password

TIP   You can also access the various web GUIs by using the drop-down menu in the upper-right corner of the web page and then clicking the **Go** button (see Figure 5-3).

NOTE   You can switch between interfaces using the same username/password combo without logging in each time. For example, if you were already logged in to the Cisco Unified Serviceability interface and switched to the Cisco Unified Reporting interface, you would not need to log in again because they use the same username and password.

The Application username is configured during installation and cannot be changed later. However, additional Application usernames can be added later. For this book, use the name appadmin for the Application username.

The Platform username is also created during the installation process. For this book, use the name osadmin for the Platform username.

Accessing the Management GUI and CLI Interfaces

This section refers to the network topology shown in Figure 5-1 and provides details about accessing and using the web management and command-line interfaces.

Accessing and Using the Web GUI

1. Using a web browser, open https://10.0.1.20/ccmadmin, and enter the Application username and password. The application username in this case is **appadmin** (see Figure 5-2).

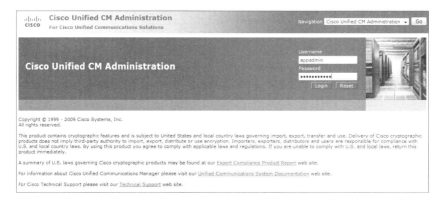

Figure 5-2 Log in to Cisco Unified Communications Manager Web Interface

2. When logged in, you can see the system version number. To jump to another management interface, use the navigation menu and click **Go** (see Figure 5-3).

Figure 5-3 Administrative Interface Navigation Menu

3. Using your mouse, you can hover over the different menu options to see the available choices.

NOTE There is a useful built-in help reference available in the Web GUI. The last choice on the menu bar is Help. The choices offered are

`Help>Contents:` Shows the contents of the Help system, Index, and Search

`Help>This Page:` Contextual information about the page you are currently viewing

`Help>About:` Displays the system version

4. To log out, use the **Logout** link under the **Go** button on the upper-right corner of the interface (see Figure 5-4).

Figure 5-4   Logging Out of Cisco Unified Communications Manager Web Interface

Accessing and Using the CLI

1. Using an SSH client, like PuTTY, open 10.0.1.20 using protocol SSH port 22 (see Figure 5-5).

Figure 5-5   SSH Client Configuration

NOTE   You may get an alert that indicates the server's key is not cached. If you trust the host, you can add the key to the Registry so that you won't get this message every time you connect (see Figure 5-6).

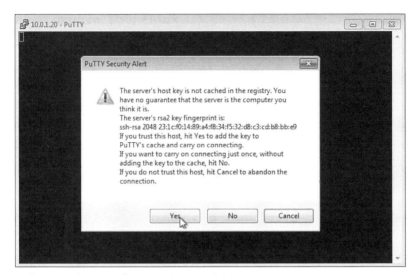

Figure 5-6 Saving the Host's Key to the Cache

2. Enter in the Platform username and password.

NOTE When you are entering the password, the cursor does not move or provide any indication that a password is being entered, even though it is.

TIP As with the Cisco IOS, you can use the built-in help to see available commands. Enter a question mark to see the available commands (see Figure 5-7).

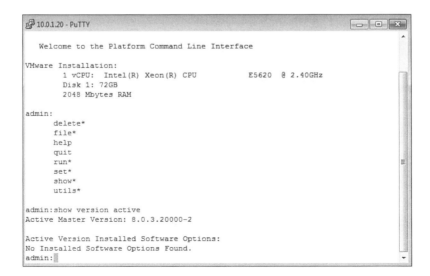

Figure 5-7 CUCM Command Line Interface (CLI)

The CLI is a powerful interface that allows an administrator to perform various system-level tasks or troubleshooting. Table 5-2 lists some common CLI commands that you should be familiar with. Refer to Chapter 8, "Management, Monitoring, and Troubleshooting CUCM," for some advanced CLI commands.

Table 5-2   Common CLI Commands

admin:?	Shows available commands.
admin:help <command>	Help for a command.
admin:show version active	Displays active system version.
admin:show version inactive	Displays if there are any other alternate versions installed. This is used when an upgrade is performed.
admin:utils service list	Displays a list of services and their status.
admin:show tech all	Displays useful information for Cisco TAC.
admin:utils network ping <IPAddress>	Pings an address and displays result.
admin:utils network traceroute <IPAddress>	Performs a traceroute to an IP address and displays result.
admin:quit	Logs you out and ends the management session.

TIP   You can press the **Tab** key to autocomplete some commands. You can also press the **up-arrow key** to recall previously entered commands.

NOTE   Complete words must be entered when issuing commands. A command like **sh tech sys hardware** will not work because it does not use the complete words.

CAUTION   Be careful when using the CLI. Some commands that can affect system stability have Are You Sure prompts, but not all. Take the time to research commands and be familiar with the effects before pressing **Enter**.

Changing CUCM Name to IP Address for DNS Independence

This section refers to the network topology shown in Figure 5-1. A common best practice is to change the system name to an IP address to mitigate issues caused by a DNS outage.

1. Using a web browser, open https://10.0.1.20/ccmadmin, and enter the Application username and password.

2. Choose **System > Server**.

3. Click the **Find** button.

4. Click the **Hostname** (see Figure 5-8).

Figure 5-8 Select a Hostname to Change

5. Change the Host Name/IP Address field to the correct IP address. In this case use 10.0.1.20. The other fields are optional, but the author usually completes the Description field as well (see Figure 5-9).

6. Click the **Save** button (see Figure 5-9).

Figure 5-9 Change the Hostname to IP Address

7. A dialog box appears to warn you that changing the name may cause problems. Because this is a new system, click **OK** to proceed (see Figure 5-10).

CAUTION If you are administering a production system, extreme care must be taken when performing certain commands. If in doubt, always check with Cisco TAC before making any systemwide changes like this.

Figure 5-10 Warning About Changing the Hostname

8. The system shows a status message indicating the success or failure of the change. You can then click the **Go** button next to the Related Links: Return to the Find/ List navigation menu to see that the change is active (see Figure 5-11).

Figure 5-11 Hostname Updated Successfully

TIP If you have another CUCM server to add, you can click the **Add New** button to add it. The author added the Subscriber (10.0.1.24) to the list of servers for use in the Unified CM Group.

9. Choose **System > Enterprise Parameters**. Scroll down to the Phone URL Parameters.

10. Change the hostname to the IP address for the following fields (see Figure 5-12):

   ▪ URL Authentication

   ▪ URL Directories

   ▪ URL Information

   ▪ URL Services

   Repeat the changes for the **Secured Phone URL Parameters** as well.

CAUTION Changes made in the Enterprise Parameters page are applied to the whole cluster. If you have any questions about clusterwide changes, contact Cisco TAC.

Figure 5-12   Updating the Hostname in the Enterprise Parameters

11. Click **Save**. Then click **Apply Config**. A window appears indicating that this change may restart all your devices (phones and gateways). Click **OK** if you want to proceed (see Figure 5-13).

Figure 5-13   Applying the Updated Configuration

Configuring a Unified CM Group

This section refers to the network topology shown in Figure 5-1 and provides configuration steps for the Unified CM Group.

1. Using a web browser, open https://10.0.1.20/ccmadmin, and enter the Application username and password.

2. Choose **System > Cisco Unified CM Group**. Click **Find**.

3. In the example, the Default group was created by the system at the time of installation. Click the **Default** link (see Figure 5-14).

Figure 5-14   Modifying the CUCM Group

4. It is a best practice to change the name to something that indicates the order of the servers available. Change the name to **CMGroup_2_1**. That name indicates that the Subscriber (2) is the first server and the Publisher (1) is the second server (see Figure 5-15).

5. To move the Subscriber from the Available Cisco Unified Communications Managers field to the Selected Cisco Unified Communications Managers field, you can either double-click the subscriber or use the down arrow located between the fields.

6. After it is moved, it will by default move to the second position. Select the Subscriber, and use the up arrow on the right side to move it up and change the order (see Figure 5-16).

7. Click **Save**. A warning appears that devices need to be reset.

8. Click the **Apply Config** button.

9. Use the **Related Links: Back to Find/List** navigation menu to return to the listing to verify that the new name is active.

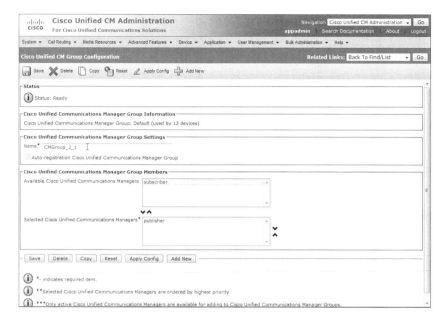

Figure 5-15   Change the Group Name

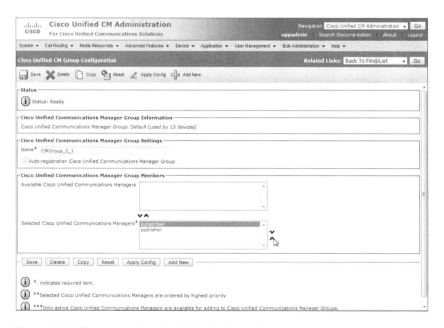

Figure 5-16   The Arrows Move the Selection Up or Down

Configuring a Phone NTP Reference

This section refers to the network topology shown in Figure 5-1. The Phone NTP Reference is used by SIP devices to determine the time. After it is configured, you can also add it to the Date/Time Group.

1. Using a web browser, open https://10.0.1.20/ccmadmin, and enter the Application username and password.

2. Choose **System** > **Phone NTP Reference**.

3. Click the **Add New** button.

4. Enter 10.0.1.1 because that is the main router that provides NTP service. Enter a description in the Description field.

5. Select **Directed Broadcast** (see Figure 5-17).

6. Click **Save**.

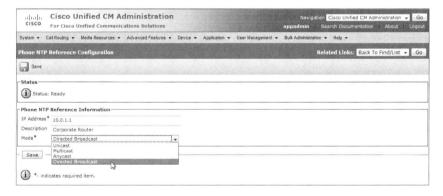

Figure 5-17   Choose Directed Broadcast

Configuring a Date/Time Group

This section details how to configure a date/time group to work for Eastern, Central, and Pacific time.

1. Using a web browser, open https://10.0.1.20/ccmadmin, and enter the Application username and password.

2. Choose **System** > **Date/Time Group**.

3. Click the **Find** button to view the current date/time group (see Figure 5-18).

4. Click **CMLocal** (the system created this during install).

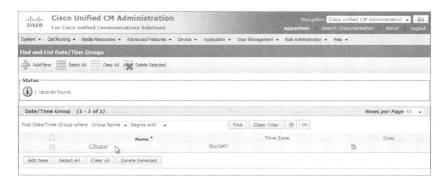

Figure 5-18   Modifying the CMLocal Date/Time Group

5. Change the Group Name field to **Eastern**.

6. In the Time Zone field, select **(GMT-5:00) America/New_York**.

NOTE   The Separator, Date Format, and Time Format settings are used to determine how the date and time display on the phone.

7. In the Time Format field, select **12-hour**.

8. In the Phone NTP References for this Date/Time Group section, click the **Add Phone NTP Reference** button. Then click the **Find** button to see available NTP References.

9. Check the box next to **10.0.1.1** for the Corporate Router NTP Reference you created earlier. Click **Add Selected** (see Figure 5-19).

10. Click the **Save** button and then the **Apply Config** button.

11. Click the **Reset** button. A warning appears because this resets all the phones using this Date/Time Group.

12. Click the **Copy** button, and change the Group Name to **Central** and the Time Zone to **(GMT-6:00) America/Chicago**.

13. Click the **Save** button and then the **Apply Config** button.

14. Click the **Copy** button, and change the Group Name to **Pacific** and the Time Zone to **(GMT-8:00) America/Los_Angeles.**

15. Click the **Save** button and then the **Apply Config** button.

16. To view the complete list, click the **Go** button next to the Related Links: Return to Find/List navigation menu (see Figure 5-20).

Figure 5-19 Selecting the NTP Reference

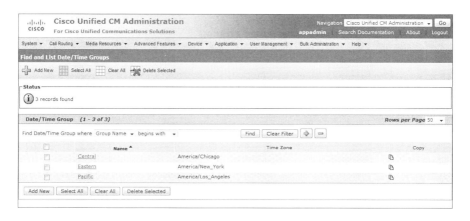

Figure 5-20 View List of Date/Time Groups

Configuring a Region

This section refers to the network topology shown in Figure 5-1 and details how to configure local and remote regions.

1. Using a web browser, open https://10.0.1.20/ccmadmin, and enter the Application username and password.

2. Choose **System > Region**.

3. Click the **Find** button to display a list of Regions. There is currently only one, Default (see Figure 5-21).

4. Click **Default**.

Figure 5-21 Changing the Default Region

5. Change the Name to **New York.**

6. Click the **Save** button. A warning appears indicating that you need to immediately reset devices (see Figure 5-22).

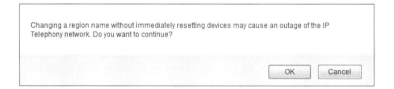

Figure 5-22 A Reminder to Perform a Device Reset

7. Click the **Apply Config** button and then the **Reset** button.

8. Click the **Add New** button (see Figure 5-23).

Figure 5-23 Add a Region

9. Enter **Chicago** in the Name field, and click the **Save** button.

10. In the Modify Relationships to Other Regions section, select **New York** and choose **8 kbps (G.729)** in the Max Audio Bit Rate column. This selection defines the codec that will be used.

11. Click **Save** (see Figure 5-24).

Figure 5-24   Choosing an Audio Codec

11. Click the **Add New** button.

12. Enter **Los Angeles** in the Name field, and click the **Save** button.

13. In the Modify Relationships to Other Regions section, select **Chicago** and choose **8 kbps (G.729)** in the Max Audio Bit Rate column. Then click **Save**.

14. In the Modify Relationships to Other Regions section, select **New York** and choose **64 kbps (G.722, G.711)** in the Max Audio Bit Rate column. Then click **Save** (see Figure 5-25).

Figure 5-25   Region Relationship Configuration

Configuring Locations

This section refers to Table 5-3 and details how to configure locations.

Table 5-3   Location Configuration Detail

Location	Los Angeles	Chicago
Connection Type	Fractional T1	SIP Trunk
Available Bandwidth	768kbps	384kbps
Region (Max Audio Bit Rate)	64kbps	8kbps
Actual Bandwidth per Call (Includes Overhead)	80kbps	24kbps
Maximum Simultaneous Calls	9	16
Location Bandwidth Setting	720kbps (9 × 80kbps)	384kbps (16 × 24kbps)

1. Using a web browser, open https://10.0.1.20/ccmadmin, and enter the Application username and password.

2. Choose **System > Location**.

3. Click the **Add New** button.

4. Enter **Los Angeles** in the Name field.

5. In the Audio Calls Information section, click the radio button next to the kbps field and enter **720**; 720kbps allows nine 64kbps voice calls to the Los Angeles location simultaneously (see Figure 5-26).

6. Click **Save**.

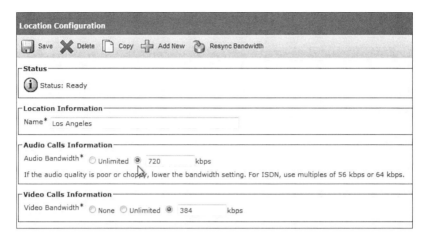

Figure 5-26   Limiting the Number of Possible Calls to a Location

7. Click the **Add New** button.

8. Enter **Chicago** in the Name field.

9. In the Audio Calls Information section, click the radio button next to the kbps field and enter **384**; 384kbps will allow sixteen 8kbps voice calls to the Chicago location simultaneously.

10. Click **Save**.

NOTE   The video bandwidth setting is the combined bandwidth for both the audio and video for a video call in that region.

Configuring Device Pools

This section refers to the network topology shown in Figure 5-1 and details how to configure Device Pools.

1. Using a web browser, open https://10.0.1.20/ccmadmin, and enter the Application username and password.

2. Choose **System > Device Pool**.

3. Click the **Find** button to list the Default Device Pool. Click **Default** to view the Device Pool properties.

4. Change the Device Pool Name to **New York Headquarters**.

5. Click **Save**.

6. Click **Copy**.

7. In the Device Pool Name field, enter **Los Angeles**.

8. Change the Date/Time Group to **Pacific**.

9. Change the Region to **Los Angeles**.

10. Change the Location to **Los Angeles** (see Figure 5-27).

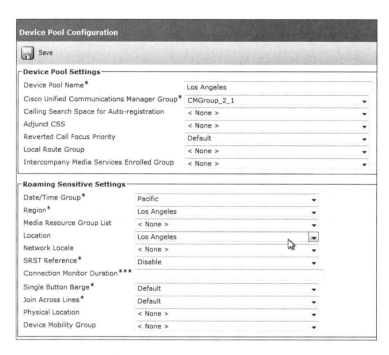

Figure 5-27   Device Pool Configuration

11. Click **Save**.

12. Click **Add New**.

13. Enter **Chicago** for the Device Pool Name.

14. For the Cisco Unified Communications Manager Group, select **CMGroup_2_1**.

15. Change the Date/Time Group to **Central**.

16. Change the Region and Location to **Chicago**.

17. Click **Save**.

Configuring a Partition

This section details how to create a Partition.

1. Using a web browser, open https://10.0.1.20/ccmadmin, and enter the Application username and password.

2. Choose **Call Routing > Class of Control > Partition**.

3. Click the **Add New** button.

NOTE   You can configure multiple Partitions at one time. Use this format, one Partition per line:

`PartitionName_PT, Partition Description`

TIP   Although a description is not a required field, it is a best practice to enter a description so that administration and troubleshooting are less complex later.

4. Enter the following values in the Name field (see Figure 5-28):

   ▪ Emergency_PT, Emergency

   ▪ Internal_PT, Internal Calls

   ▪ Local_PT, Local Calls

   ▪ Toll_PT, Long Distance

   ▪ Intl_PT, International Calls

   ▪ NewYork_PT, New York Devices

   ▪ Chicago_PT, Chicago Devices

   ▪ LosAngeles_PT, Los Angeles Devices

5. Click the **Save** button.

Figure 5-28   Create the Partitions

Configuring a Calling Search Space

1. Using a web browser, open https://10.0.1.20/ccmadmin, and enter the Application username and password.

2. Choose **Call Routing > Class of Control > Calling Search Space**.

3. Click the **Add New** button.

4. Enter **Manager_CSS** in the Name field and **Manager** in the Description field.

5. Select **Emergency_PT** from the Available Partitions field, and use the down arrow between the two fields to move **Emergency_PT** to the Selected Partitions field.

6. Select **NewYork_PT** and move it to the Selected Partitions field (see Figure 5-29).

NOTE The order within the Selected Partitions is important to call handling. You can use the up/down arrows to the right of the Selected Partitions field to change the order of the list.

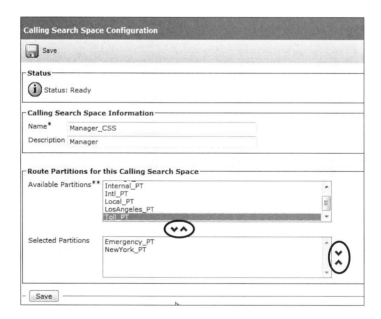

Figure 5-29 Adding Partitions to a CSS

7. Create the following according to Table 5-4. Use the **Add New** button to add more Calling Search Spaces.

Table 5-4   Calling Search Space Configuration

Name	Description	Selected Partitions (In Order)
Manager_CSS	Manager	Emergency_PT Internal_PT NewYork_PT LosAngeles_PT Chicago_PT Local_PT Toll_PT Intl_PT
Employees_CSS	Employees	Emergency_PT Internal_PT NewYork_PT LosAngeles_PT Chicago_PT Local_PT
Lobby_CSS	Lobby and Wall Phones	Emergency_PT Internal_PT Local_PT

Activating Services and Features

This section provides details about how to activate services on the CUCM cluster to support calling features.

1. Using a web browser, open https://10.0.1.20/ccmservice (or use the main Navigation menu; see Figure 5-30) and enter the Application username and password.

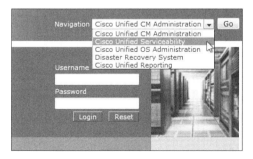

Figure 5-30   Using the Navigation Menu

2. Choose **Tools > Service Activation**.

3. Select the server you would like to activate services on, and click the **Go** button (see Figure 5-31).

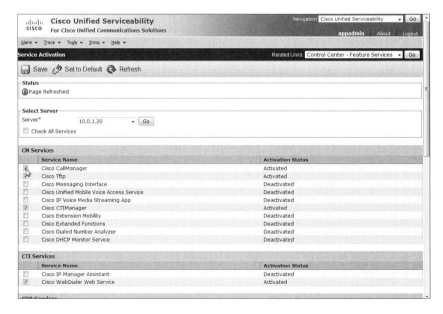

Figure 5-31 Select the Server to Activate Services On

NOTE If you have only one server, a Publisher, you can choose the **Set to Default** button. That activates only the services a standalone Publisher requires.

If you have a cluster, the Publisher and Subscriber(s) in your cluster have different service activation requirements. There are some services that should run only the Publisher, and some services that should run only on Subscriber servers. If you have questions, open a support case with Cisco TAC or review the documentation at http://www.cisco.com/en/US/docs/voice_ip_comm/cucm/service/8_0_1/admin/sasrvact.html#wp1098401.

TIP A best practice is to activate only the services that you need. Additional, unused services can negatively affect call processing because of unnecessary processes consuming memory and CPU cycles.

4. Check the box next to the service(s) you want to activate, and click **Save** (see Figure 5-32).

Figure 5-32 Activating Services on the CUCM

Creating a Phone Button Template

This section refers to Table 5-5 and describes how to modify a Phone Button Template.

Table 5-5   Phone Button Template Sample Requirements

User Type	Phone Type	Buttons Required
Manager	7971 SCCP 8 Buttons	Line 1 Line 2 Line 3 Do Not Disturb Mobility Intercom Speed Dial BLF

1. Using a web browser, open https://10.0.1.20/ccmadmin, and enter the Application username and password.

2. Choose **Device > Device Settings > Phone Button Template**.

3. Click the **Find** button to see the default Phone Button Templates.

NOTE   Cisco includes many prebuilt Phone Button Templates that should be sufficient in most situations. Creating a new template may be necessary if you have a phone with an expansion module and need to add more lines, or if you would like to have features other than lines available on a particular set of devices.

4. Because you are making a custom 7971 Phone Button Template, click the **Add New** button.

5. From the drop-down menu, select **Standard 7971 SCCP**, and click the **Copy** button.

TIP   You can also press the **Copy** button on the listing of Phone Button Templates (see Figure 5-33).

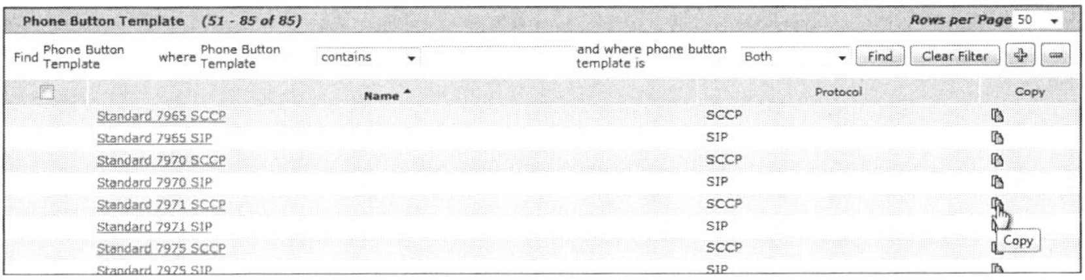

Figure 5-33   Copying a Phone Button Template

6. Change the Button Template Name to **Manager 7971 SCCP**, and click the **Save** button.

7. Use the drop-down menus in the Feature column to select the required buttons (see Figure 5-34).

8. Click the **Save** button.

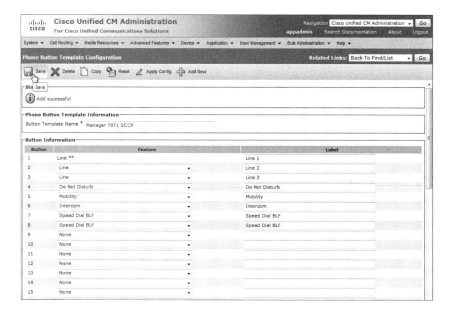

Figure 5-34   Phone Button Template

Creating a Softkey Template

This section provides details about how to configure a Softkey Template.

1. Using a web browser, open https://10.0.1.20/ccmadmin, and enter the Application username and password.

2. Choose **Device > Device Settings > Softkey Template**.

3. Click the **Find** button to see a list of Default templates.

4. Click the **Copy** button in the same row as the Standard Manager.

5. Change the Name field to **Manager New York**, and change the Description to **New York Manager Phone**.

6. Click **Save**.

7. In the Related Links navigation menu, select **Configure Softkey Layout**, and click the **Go** button (see Figure 5-35).

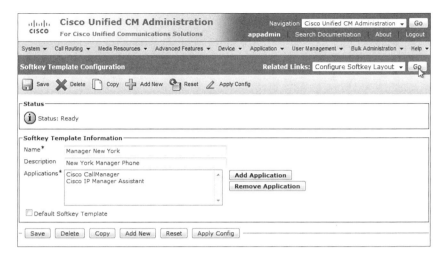

Figure 5-35   Configuring the Softkey Layout

8. Use the drop-down menu to select which call state to configure. Select **Ring In** (see Figure 5-36).

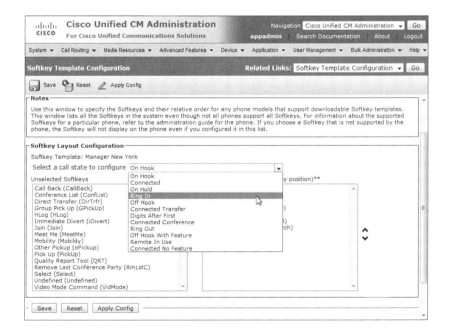

Figure 5-36   Configuring a Call State

9. From the Unselected Softkeys field, select **Immediate Divert (iDivert)**. Use the arrow (>) between the fields to move the selection to the Selected Softkeys field.

When an incoming call arrives that the user does not want to answer, iDivert sends the call directly into a configured voice-messaging system. Users love this feature!

10. Select **Immediate Divert (iDivert)** and use the up arrow to move the selection to position three (see Figure 5-37).

TIP   The **Undefined (Undefined)** softkey is actually a placeholder or blank softkey. This is useful when you want to configure a blank softkey to prevent accidental presses to adjacent softkeys. For example, you wouldn't want to configure the Answer softkey adjacent to the iDivert softkey because users might accidentally press the iDivert key when they actually meant to answer the call.

11. Click **Save**.

12. You can now choose another call state to modify. Always click the **Save** button before configuring another call state, or your changes will be lost.

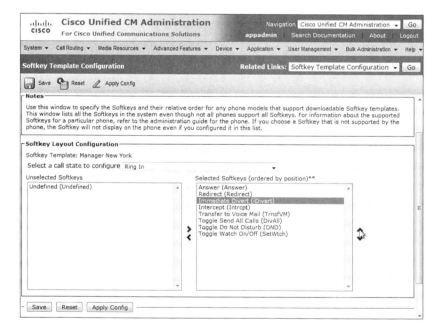

Figure 5-37   Changing the Softkey Order

Creating a Common Phone Profile

This section details how to create a Common Phone Profile.

1. Using a web browser, open https://10.0.1.20/ccmadmin, and enter the Application username and password.

2. Choose **Device > Device Settings > Common Phone Profile**.

3. Click the **Add New** button.

4. In the Name field, enter **Managers**.

5. In the Description field, enter **Managers**.

6. Scroll down to the Product Specific Configuration Layout section. Here you can view/modify settings that affect how the phone functions.

7. Find Settings Access and change it to **Restricted.** This setting enables the user to change settings such as ringtone and display contrast, but it doesn't enable them to view network settings or other sensitive information. This setting is especially important for phones that the public might use, such as lobby phones. A great deal can be learned about your network from access to the settings on the phone (see Figure 5-38).

NOTE Restricted settings access can also hinder troubleshooting the device in some cases. For example, if the phone were no longer registering with the CUCM, you couldn't view the network settings if the Settings Access were set to Restricted on that phone the last time it successfully registered because that setting is cached on the phone.

8. Click **Save**.

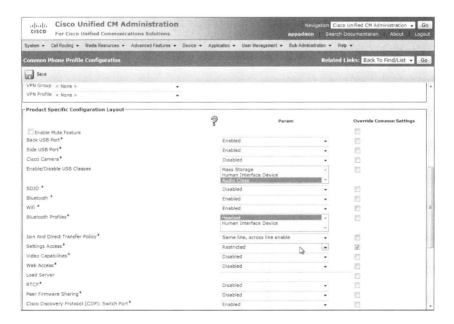

Figure 5-38 Common Phone Profile

Creating an Application User with Administrative Rights

This section details how to create another application user. The application user has access to the administration interface of the CUCM and can perform administrative tasks.

NOTE   It is considered a best practice to give each administrator a unique user ID.

CAUTION   The Application username and password defined at system install is a member of the Standard CCM Super Users group. It is a good idea to perform daily administrative tasks using an account with fewer privileges to protect against inadvertent modifications. This section creates a user belonging to the Standard CCM Users group.

1. Using a web browser, open https://10.0.1.20/ccmadmin, and enter the Application username and password.

2. Choose **User Management > Application User**.

3. Click the **Find** button to view a list of available application users. The system defines some application users during install and when services are activated. You should not modify them.

4. Click the **Copy** icon next to the username appadmin (see Figure 5-39).

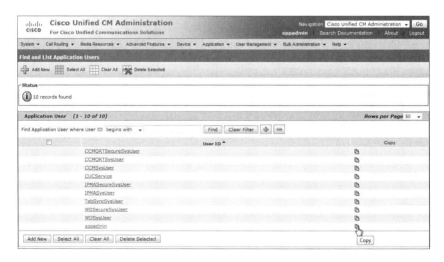

Figure 5-39   Application User Listing

5. Enter **tech** in the User ID field.

6. Enter the new user's password in the Password and Confirm Password fields.

7. In the Permissions Information section, select **Standard CCM Super Users** and click the **Remove from User Group** button (see Figure 5-40).

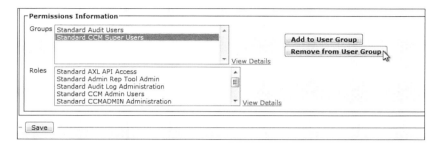

Figure 5-40 Modifying Application User Group Membership

  8. Click the **Add to User Group** button.

  9. Click the **Find** button; then check the box next to **Standard CCM Admin Users**.

  10. Click the **Add Selected** button (see Figure 5-41).

  11. Click the **Save** button.

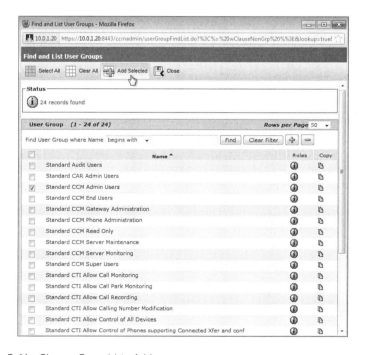

Figure 5-41 Choose Group(s) to Add

Creating an Application User with Read-Only Rights

This section details how to create an application user with read-only access.

1. Using a web browser, open https://10.0.1.20/ccmadmin, and enter the Application username and password.
2. Choose **User Management > Application User**.
3. Click the **Add New** button.
4. Enter **readonly** in the User ID field.
5. Enter the new user's password in the Password and Confirm Password fields.
6. In the Permissions Information section, click the **Add to User Group** button.
7. Check the box next to **Standard CCM Read Only**.
8. Click the **Add Selected** button.
9. Click the **Save** button.

Creating an End User Manually

This section refers to Table 5-6 and details the steps needed to add an end user.

Table 5-6   Password and PIN Usage

Type	Purpose
Password	Allows access to the user web pages
PIN	Used for phone-based applications, such as voicemail

1. Using a web browser, open https://10.0.1.20/ccmadmin, and enter the Application username and password.
2. Choose **User Management > End User**.
3. Click the **Add New** button.
4. Enter **First Last** in the User ID field.
5. Enter a password in the Password field.
6. Enter a PIN in the PIN field.
7. Enter **Last** in the Last Name field.
8. Enter **1001** in the Telephone Number field.
9. Click **Save**.

NOTE   The Permissions Information section does not appear until the new user's profile is saved. Users will not have access to the user web pages if they are not assigned to the proper User Group.

10. In the Permission Information section, click the **Add to User Group** button.

11. Check the box next to the **Standard CCM End Users**.

12. Click the **Add Selected** button.

13. Click the **Save** button (see Figure 5-42).

Figure 5-42   End User Details

TIP   Users can now log in to manage their own settings at https://<IPAddress>/ ccmuser with their user ID and password (see Figure 5-43).

Figure 5-43   End Users Can Log In to the CCMUSER Interface

Adding Users via LDAP Synchronization

This section refers to the network topology in Figure 5-1 and Table 5-7 and details the steps needed to perform LDAP Synchronization.

CAUTION   Enabling LDAP Synchronization disables any users that were added by other means. It also disables the ability to add or delete any users because LDAP is used. The telephone PIN and password are still maintained in the CUCM database though.

Table 5-7   LDAP Configuration Details

`LDAP Configuration Name:` `Corporate LDAP`	Name used in CUCM to identify this LDAP Directory
`LDAP Manager Distinguished` `Name: mike@voicepcg.local`	User with administrative rights to LDAP
`User Search Base: cn=Users,` `dc=voicepcg, dc=local`	Defines where CUCM looks for users
`LDAP Server Information>IP` `Address: 10.0.1.23`	Defines the IP address of the LDAP server

1. Activate the **Cisco DirSync** service on the Publisher. (Refer to the "Activating Services and Features" section.)

2. Using a web browser, open https://10.0.1.20/ccmadmin, and enter the Application username and password.

3. Choose **System > LDAP > LDAP System**.

4. Check the box for **Enable Synchronizing from LDAP Server**, and click the **Save** button (see Figure 5-44).

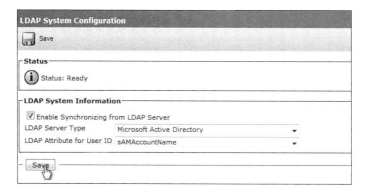

Figure 5-44   LDAP System Information

5. Choose **System > LDAP > LDAP Directory**.

6. Click the **Add New** button.

7. Enter **Corporate LDAP** in the LDAP Configuration Name field.

8. Enter **mike@voicepcg.local** in the LDAP Manager Distinguished Name field. This user must have administrative access to the LDAP database. Typically, you would create an account in the domain for CUCM to use for LDAP synchronization.

9. Enter **mike@voicepcg.local**'s password twice.

10. Enter **cn=Users**, **dc=voicepcg**, and **dc=local** in the LDAP User Search Base. If you have a question about your specific User Search Base, check with your LDAP administrator.

11. Check the box next to **Perform Sync Just Once**.

12. Enter **10.0.1.23** in the Host Name or IP Address for Server field (see Figure 5-45).

13. Click **Save**.

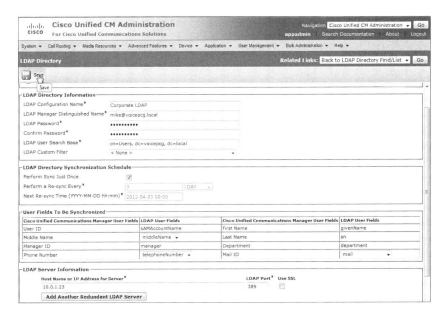

Figure 5-45 LDAP Directory Settings

14. After the page refreshes, click the **Perform Full Sync Now** button (see Figure 5-46).

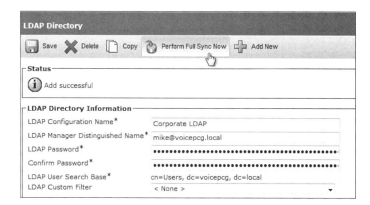

Figure 5-46   LDAP Synchronization

15. Allow a few moments for the synchronization to complete, and then choose **User Management > End User** to view the results of the synchronization (see Figure 5-47).

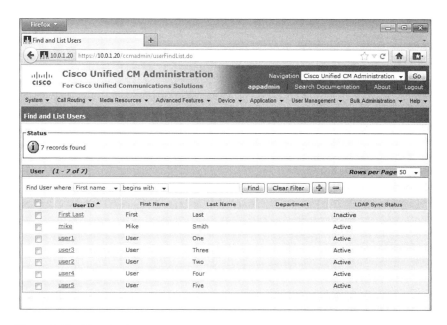

Figure 5-47   View the Results of the LDAP Sync

Configuring LDAP Authentication for End Users

This section details the steps needed to enable LDAP Authentication for End Users. This allows users to authenticate to the user web pages using their LDAP username and password.

1. Using a web browser, open https://10.0.1.20/ccmadmin, and enter the Application username and password.

2. Choose **System** > **LDAP** > **LDAP Authentication**.

3. Check the box for **Use LDAP Authentication for End Users**.

4. Enter **mike@voicepcg.local** for the LDAP Manager Distinguished Name.

5. Enter the password twice.

6. Enter **cn=Users, dc=voicepcg, dc=local** in the LDAP User Search Base. If you have a question about your specific User Search Base, check with your LDAP administrator.

7. Enter **10.0.1.23** in the Host Name or IP Address for Server field (see Figure 5-48).

8. Click **Save**.

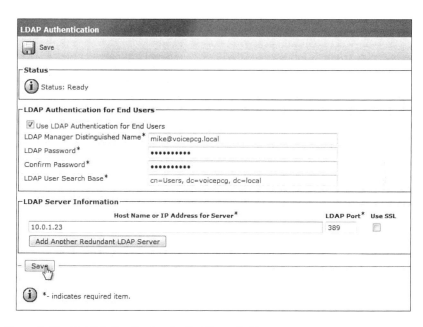

Figure 5-48   LDAP Authentication for End Users Settings

Adding an IP Phone to CUCM Manually

This section refers to the Topology in Figure 5-1 and details the steps needed to add a phone manually to CUCM.

1. Using a web browser, open https://10.0.1.20/ccmadmin, and enter the Application username and password.

2. Choose **Device** > **Phone** and click the **Add New** button.

3. Select **Phone Type Cisco 7971** and click **Next**.

4. Select the **device protocol SCCP** and click **Next**.

5. Enter **00070E16506D** (the 7971's MAC address) in the MAC Address field.

NOTE   The MAC address can be found on the bottom of the phone or on the box the phone came in.

6. Enter **1001 Smith, Mike** in the Description field.

7. Select **New York Headquarters** for the Device Pool.

8. Select **Manager New York** for the Softkey Template.

9. Select **Manager 7971 SCCP** for the Phone Button Template.

10. Select **Managers** for the Common Phone Profile.

11. Select **mike** as the Owner User ID.

12. In the Protocol Specific Information section, select **Cisco 7971 – Standard SCCP Non-Secure Profile** as the Device Security Profile.

13. Click the **Save** button, and then click the **Apply Config** button as prompted (see Figure 5-49).

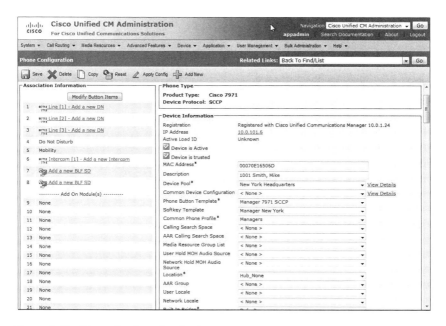

Figure 5-49   Phone Configuration Settings

Adding a Directory Number (DN) to a Phone

This section refers to the topology in Figure 5-1 and configuration options shown in Table 5-8 and shows the steps needed to add a DN to a phone. Although there are many configurable options for a DN, Table 5-8 includes the options you will use.

Table 5-8   Phone DN Configuration Options

Option	Description
Directory Number	This is the extension of the phone.
Route Partition	Assign the extension to a partition.
Description	This description is not displayed to the user.
Alerting Name	Displays the called party's name on the calling party's device.
ASCII Alerting Name	The same as above except this is for devices that don't understand Unicode (Internationalized) characters.
Calling Search Space	Assign a Calling Search Space (CSS) to the extension.
Display (Internal Caller ID)	Displays the calling party's name to the called party.
ASCII Display (Internal Caller ID)	The same as above except this is for devices that don't understand Unicode (Internationalized) characters.
Line Text Label	Determines what is displayed next to the line button on supported devices.
ASCII Line Text Label	The same as the preceding except this is for devices that don't understand Unicode (Internationalized) characters.
External Phone Number Mask	Displays the complete phone number on the display of supported devices. If nothing is entered, the Directory Number will be shown. If the extension number is 1000 and the External Phone Number Mask is 212555XXXX, then 2125551000 would be displayed on the device and sent as the caller ID on outbound calls if configured properly.

1. Using a web browser, open https://10.0.1.20/ccmadmin, and enter the Application username and password.

2. Choose **Device > Phone**, and click the **Find** button to list all the phones available.

3. Click the link in the Device Name(Line) column SEP00070E16506D.

4. Click the first link on the left side labeled **Line[1] – Add a new DN** (see Figure 5-50).

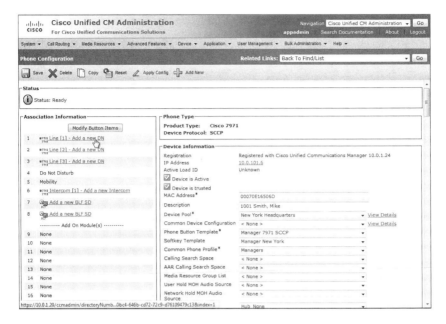

Figure 5-50   Adding a Directory Number

5. Enter **1001** in the Directory Number field.

6. Select **NewYork_PT** for Route Partition.

7. Enter **1001 Smith, Mike** in the Description, Alerting Name, and ASCII Alerting Name fields (see Table 5-8 for more information).

8. Select **Manager_CSS** for the Calling Search Space (see Figure 5-51).

9. To forward calls to voicemail when the line is busy or not answered, check the boxes in the Voice Mail column for **Forward Busy Internal, Forward Busy External, Forward No Answer Internal**, and **Forward No Answer External.** The Forward Unregistered Internal and Forward Unregistered External boxes are checked for you automatically.

10. Scroll down to the section titled Line 1 on Device SEP00070E16506D.

11. Enter **1001 Smith, Mike** in the Display (Internal Caller ID) and ASCII Display (Internal Caller ID) fields (see Table 5-8 for more information).

12. Enter **Private Line 1001** in the Line Text Label and ASCII Line Text Label fields.

13. Enter **212555XXXX** in the External Phone Number Mask field (see Figure 5-52).

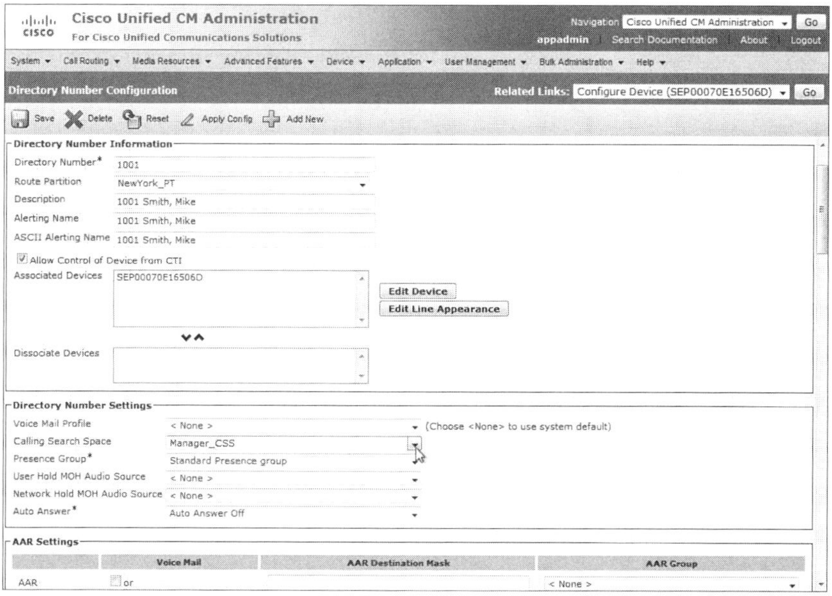

Figure 5-51   Directory Number Details

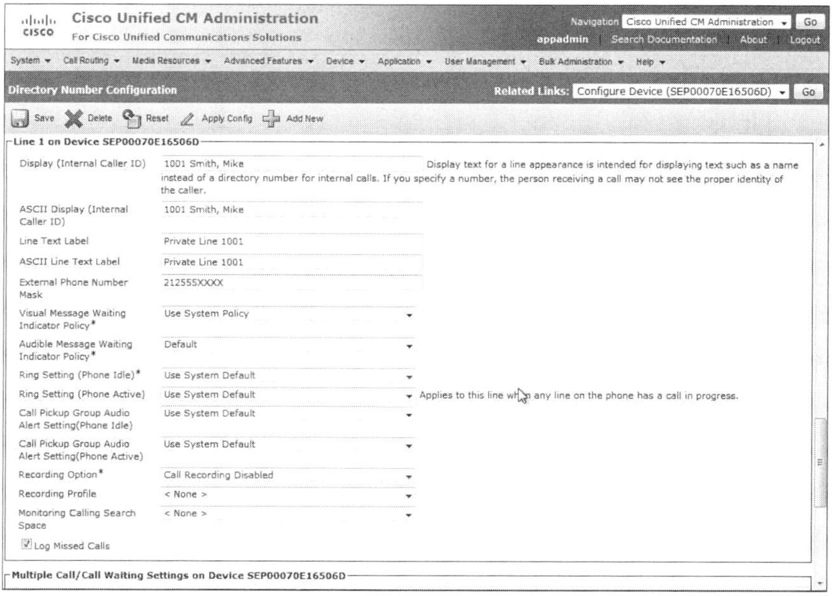

Figure 5-52   Line 1 Details

14. Click the **Save** button and then the **Apply Config** button.

15. To go back to the main device page, you can click the **Go** button on the Related Links navigation menu.

Adding Phones Using Auto-registration

This section details the steps needed to allow phones to register automatically using Auto-registration.

1. Using a web browser, open https://10.0.1.20/ccmadmin, and enter the Application username and password.

2. Choose **System > Cisco Unified CM**, and click the **Find** button to list the available servers.

3. Click the link for **subscriber**.

4. Enter **1070** in the Ending Directory Number field.

5. Enter **1060** in the Starting Directory Number field.

NOTE   The check box for **Auto-registration Disabled on This Cisco Unified Communications Manager** automatically unchecks itself when you change the Ending Directory Number field.

6. Select **Internal_PT** for the Partition. This allows any automatically registered phones to make internal calls only.

7. Click **Save** and then the **Apply Config** (see Figure 5-53).

8. You can verify that Auto-registration is working by choosing **Device > Phone** and then clicking the **Find** button. If you see phones registered with a Description of Auto 106X, you know it is working (see Figure 5-54).

Figure 5-53 Auto-Registration Configuration

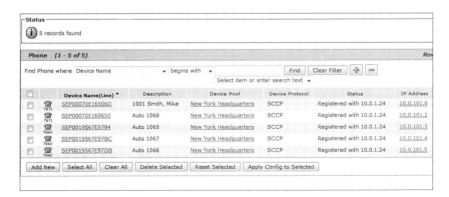

Figure 5-54 View the Results of Auto-Registration

Adding End Users and Phones with the Bulk Administration Tool (BAT)

This section describes how to import multiple users and phones using the Bulk Administration Tool.

NOTE   The Bulk Administration Tool requires Microsoft Excel with macros enabled for BAT to work correctly.

TIP   When importing Phones using BAT, you can import PHONES OF THE SAME TYPE ONLY in the same file. You cannot mix phone types in one BAT import. Phone types are 7971, 7975, 6921, and so on.

NOTE   You import three phones and users in the following example. Normally, you wouldn't use BAT to import three phones and users because there are so many steps involved. BAT is powerful and can be a time-saver when you have many phones and users to import, so the example provided here should be enough to get you started with BAT.

1. Using a web browser, open https://10.0.1.20/ccmadmin, and enter the Application username and password.

2. Choose **Bulk Administration > Upload/Download Files**.

3. Click the **Find** button; then check the box for bat.xlt, and click **Download Selected**. Open **bat.xlt** with Excel, and click the **Enable Content (macros),** if needed (see Figure 5-55).

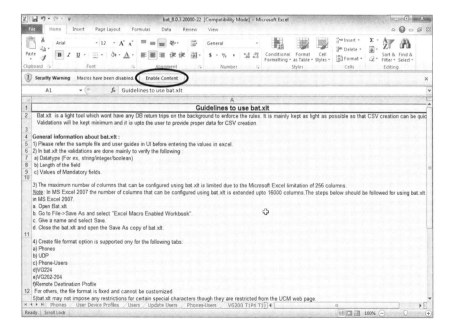

Figure 5-55   Enable Macros to Edit the BAT File

4. On the bottom of the spreadsheet are tabs indicating the types of imports that can be done. Choose the **Phones-Users** tab (see Figure 5-56).

5. The columns indicate which information is MANDATORY.

6. Enter **First Name** (Column A), **Last Name** (Column B). and **UserID** (Column C).

7. Scroll right to **MAC Address** (Column X), and enter valid MAC addresses and **Description** (Column Y) (see Figure 5-56).

8. Check the **Dummy MAC Address** so that BAT creates fake MAC addresses if you do not have the phones yet with the real MAC addresses.

TIP   You can add more columns, such as CSS, Device Pool, and lines by clicking the **Create File Format** button.

9. Click the **Export to BAT Format** button (see Figure 5-56).

Figure 5-56   Enter Details into the BAT File and Then Export

10. Save the file using a name that makes sense for what you are doing, such as 7940_bat.txt.

Before you can import the BAT file, you need to create a Phone Template.

1. Choose **Bulk Administration > Phones > Phone Template**, and click the **Add New** button.

2. This process is the same as adding a new phone. From the drop-down menu, choose the **Phone Type Cisco 7940**; click **Next**.

3. Select the **Device Protocol SCCP** and click **Next**.

4. Enter **7940_Bulk_Import** in the Template Name field.

5. Enter **7940 Import** in the Description field.

6. Select **New York Headquarters** for the Device Pool.

7. Select **Standard 7940 SCCP** for the Phone Button Template.

8. Select **Standard User** for the Softkey Template.

9. For the Device Security Profile, select **Cisco 7940 – Standard SCCP Non-Secure Profile**.

10. Click **Save**.

The page refreshes and the Association Information section appears. You can create a Line Template by clicking **Line[1] — Add a New DN**. This creates common settings for all DNs to be added later.

1. To create a User Template, choose **Bulk Administration > Users > User Template**.

2. Click the **Add New** button.

3. In the User Template Name field, enter **users_bat**.

4. Enter any other information you would like all the users to have in the appropriate fields.

5. Click **Save**. Upload the BAT file to CUCM.

6. Choose **Bulk Administration > Upload/Download Files**.

7. Click the **Add New** button.

8. In the File field, browse to the location where you saved your BAT file.

9. For Select The Target, select **Phones/users** (see Figure 5-57).

10. For the Select Transaction Type, select **Insert Phones/users**.

11. Click **Save**.

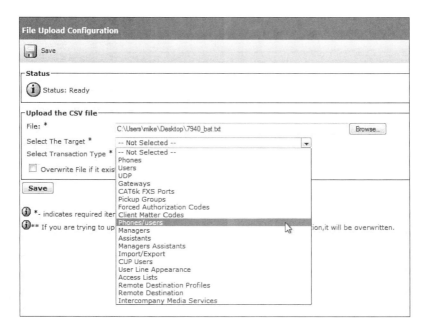

Figure 5-57 Uploading the BAT File

Begin the import process by first validating the file to make sure that the import will be successful.

1. Choose **Bulk Administration** > **Phones & Users** > **Validate Phones/Users**.

2. File Name: **7940_bat.txt**.

3. Phone Template Name: **7940_Bulk_Import**.

4. Job Description: **Validate Phones/Users** (see Figure 5-58).

5. Click **Submit**.

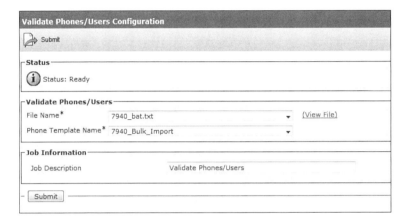

Figure 5-58   Validate the BAT File

The job is now sent to the scheduler to be run when the system deems appropriate. Normally, it is processed immediately, but it depends on the current load on the server.

1. Choose **Bulk Administration** > **Job Scheduler**.

2. Click on the **Job Id** link (see Figure 5-59).

3. Look in the Job Result Status column to make sure that the validation was successful.

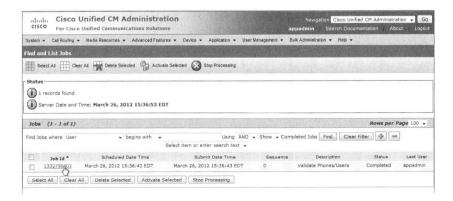

Figure 5-59   View the Results of the Validation

Use BAT to import the phones and users into the system.

4. Choose **Bulk Administration** > **Phones & Users** > **Insert Phones with Users**.

5. Complete this form in a similar manner to the validation step, and click **Submit**.

6. Use the Job Scheduler to view the status of the job. If there are errors, view the Log File to determine what failed.

7. Choose **Device** > **Phone** and click the **Find** button to verify that the phones now appear (see Figure 5-60).

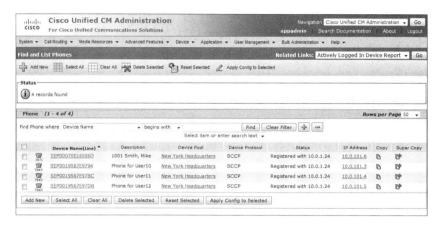

Figure 5-60   Verify the Phones Were Added

Configuring an H.323 Gateway in CUCM

This section provides the steps to create an H.323 for PSTN connectivity.

1. Using a web browser, open https://10.0.1.20/ccmadmin, and enter the Application username and password.

2. Choose **Device** > **Gateway**.

3. Click the **Add New** button.

4. Select **H.323 Gateway** as the Gateway Type from the drop-down menu (see Figure 5-61).

5. Use the IP address as the Device Name: **10.0.1.1**.

6. Enter **New York Gateway** in the Description field.

7. Select **New York Headquarters** as the Device Pool.

8. Click **Save**; then **Apply Config** as prompted.

NOTE   The gateway device must have the required PSTN or SIP interfaces and be configured for gateway service for calls to actually be processed.

Figure 5-61 Adding an H.323 Gateway

Configuring a Route Pattern

This section refers to Table 5-9 and Table 5-10 and lists the steps needed to configure a route pattern.

Table 5-9 Wildcards in Route Patterns, Examples, and Results

Wildcard	Description	Example	Result/Use
X	Single digit 0 through 9.	5X	Matches 50 through 59
.	(Period or dot) indicates Access Code Termination.	9.555XXXX	Dial 9 "to get an outside line" and then a local 555 number
[A–D]	Indicates a single digit (0–9) from the brackets either in a range or individually specified.	[45-7]XXX	4000 through 4999 5000 through 5999 6000 through 6999 7000 through 7999
[^A–D]	Indicates a single digit (0–9) not included in the brackets in a range or individually specified.	[^12-59]XXX	6000 through 6999 7000 through 7999 8000 through 8999

Wildcard	Description	Example	Result/Use
!	Matches at least one digit up to any number of digits until the T302 timer expires. (The T302 interdigit timeout is specified in the Cisco CallManager Service Parameter. Default is 15 seconds.)	877!	8773 8779004 8775558876 877555555000555
#	Terminates Interdigit Time-out—sends the call right away instead of waiting for the T302 timer to expire.	9.011!#	9.0115551212# User dials the # key to send the call immediately
@	North American Dial Plan.	9.@	9.5551212 9.18005551212

Table 5-10   Some Typical Route Patterns

Route Pattern	Description
911	911 Emergency Services
9.911	911 Emergency Services (user dialed 9 first)
9.411	411 Directory Services
9.[2-9]XXXXXX	Local seven-digit call
9.1[2-9]XX[2-9]XXXXXX	Long Distance or Toll Free
9.011!	International
9.011#	International

1. Using a web browser, open https://10.0.1.20/ccmadmin, and enter the Application username and password.

2. Choose **Call Routing > Route/Hunt > Route Pattern**.

3. Click **Add New**.

4. Enter **9.[2-9]XXXXXX** as the Route Pattern. Table 5-10 lists this as a local seven-digit pattern.

5. Select **NewYork_PT** for the Partition. This allows other devices (phones) in the NewYork_PT partition to use this route pattern.

6. Select **10.0.1.1** in the Gateway/Route List drop-down menu (see Figure 5-62).

7. Scroll down to the Called Party Transformations section. Select **PreDot** in the Discard Digits field. This strips the 9 before sending the dialed digits to the gateway for handling.

8. Click **Save**.

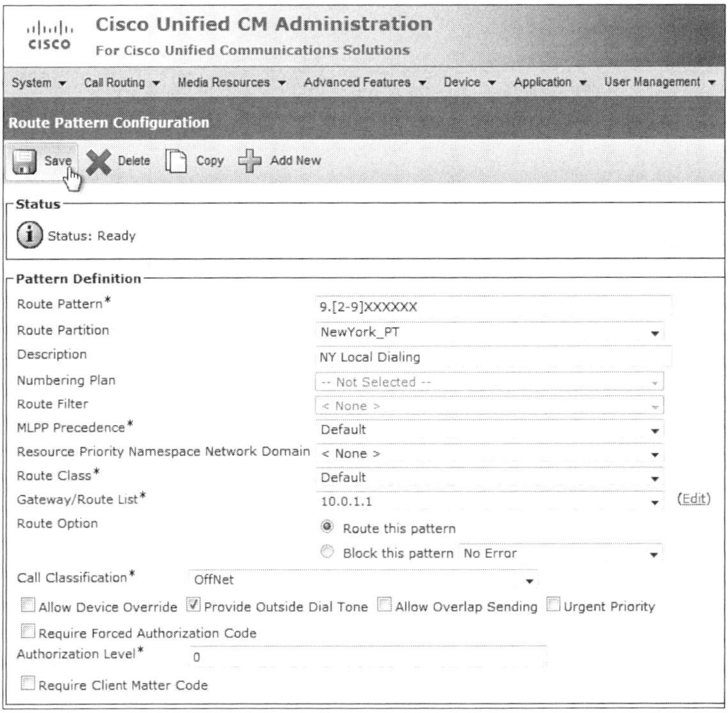

Figure 5-62 Route Pattern Configuration Details

CHAPTER 6

Cisco Unified Communications Manager (CUCM) Telephony and Mobility Features

This chapter provides information and commands concerning the following topics:

- Configuring a Hunt Group
- Configuring Shared Lines
- Configuring Barge and Privacy
- Configuring Call Forward
- Configuring Call Pickup
- Configuring Call Park
- Configuring Directed Call Park
- Configuring Native Presence (Busy Lamp Field [BLF] Speed Dial)
- Configuring Extension Mobility
- Configuring Intercom
- Configuring Mobile Connect
- Configuring Mobile Voice Access (MVA)

Topology

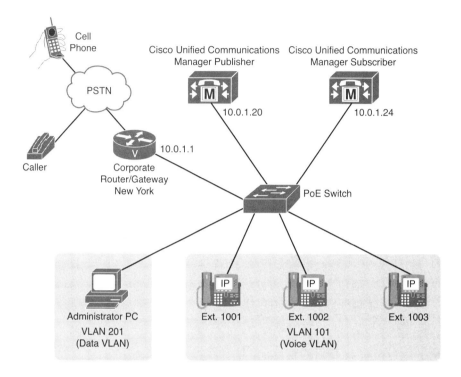

Figure 6-1   Topology

Configuring a Hunt Group

This section refers to the network topology shown in Figure 6-1 and provides configuration steps for a Hunt Group. There are three tasks you need to complete to configure a Hunt Group. (See Table 6-1.)

Table 6-1   Hunt Group Tasks

1. Create a Line Group	Configure hunt options and assign Directory Numbers (DN).
2. Create a Hunt List	Assign Line Groups.
3. Create a Hunt Pilot	The number callers use to access the Hunt Group.

Configuring a Line Group

1. Using a web browser, open https://10.0.1.20/ccmadmin, and enter the Application username and password.

2. Choose **Call Routing > Route/Hunt > Line Group**. Click the **Add New** button.

3. Enter **Marketing_LG** as the Hunt Group name.

4. Enter **12** as the RNA Reversion Timeout. This value determines how many seconds CUCM allows a phone to ring before trying the next destination.

5. Select **Circular** as the Distribution Algorithm.

NOTE There are four Distribution Algorithms to choose from. See Table 6-2 for a description of each.

Table 6-2 Distribution Algorithm Descriptions

Line Group Members Example (From Figure 6-3)	
Selected DN/Route Partition	1003/NewYork_PT 1001/NewYork_PT 1002/NewYork_PT
Distribution Algorithm	**Description**
Top Down	This method distributes calls to idle and available members of a Line Group in the order they are listed in the Selected DN/Route Partition field. Using the previous example, DN 1003 would be the first to get a call, then 1001, and finally 1002. If 1003 just got off a call and another call came in, 1003 would get that call even though it just finished with a call. This algorithm is used where you want 1003 to take the majority of the calls, whereas 1002 and 1001 would take calls only if 1003 is busy.
Circular	This method distributes calls to idle and available members of a Line Group in the order they are listed in the Selected DN/Route Partition field in a rotating manner. Using the previous example, DN 1003 would be first, then 1001, and finally 1002. The Circular algorithm keeps track of which DN just took a call and then distributes the next call to the next available and idle DN. So if DN 1003 and 1001 just finished up a call and are available and idle, CUCM would still distribute the next call to 1002. This algorithm is useful if you want calls to be delivered to members equally.
Longest Idle Time	This method distributes calls to idle and available members of a Line Group starting with those that have been idle the longest to the least idle member. Using the previous example, if DN 1001 and 1002 just finished with calls while 1003 has been idle for a while, then 1003 would get the next call. This algorithm is useful when you have members of a line group that handle calls quickly and thus seem to get all the calls in a Top Down or Circular algorithm. With the Longest Idle Time algorithm, calls are more fairly distributed possibly allowing the members more time between calls.

Line Group Members Example (From Figure 6-3)	
Broadcast	This method distributes calls to all idle and available members of a Line Group at the same time. All idle or available DNs in a group would ring at the same time allowing each member an opportunity to answer the call.
	TIP This algorithm is useful for sales and customer service areas to ensure that a call is answered as quickly as possible.

6. Leave the default selection for the No Answer Hunt Option. This setting enables CUCM to try to send the call to available members, and if none answer, then send the call to the next Line Group in a Hunt List. This is useful when you have multiple Line Groups to provide overflow and coverage destinations.

7. Select **Try Next Member, but Do Not Go to the Next Group** as the Busy Hunt Option. This setting enables the CUCM to try another available station if the first station is busy. The call does not move to the next group in this case; instead it stops hunting if the last member is busy or unavailable.

8. Select **Stop Hunting** as the Not Available Hunt Option. The CUCM stops hunting if the first member is not available. This is useful where you have a group that always has the first member available, like a help desk, during normal business hours. So with this setting, if that first member is Not Available, the CUCM sends the call to a destination defined in the Hunt Pilot configuration.

9. Select **NewYork_PT** as the Partition to choose Directory Numbers from. Click the **Find** button.

10. Choose 1001, 1002, and 1003, and click the **Add to Line Group** button. (See Figure 6-2.)

11. The Directory Numbers move to the Current Line Group Members – Selected DN/Route Partition field. This field is an ordered list that determines the hunt order. Select **DN 1003** and use the ↑ arrow to the right to change DN 1003 to the first position. (See Figure 6-3.)

12. Click **Save**.

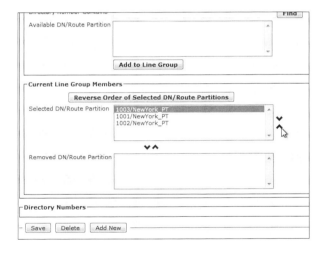

Line Group Information

Line Group Name*   Marketing_LG

RNA Reversion Timeout*   12

Distribution Algorithm*   Circular

Hunt Options

No Answer*   Try next member; then, try next group in Hunt List

Busy**   Try next member, but do not go to next group

Not Available**   Stop hunting

Line Group Member Information

Find Directory Numbers to Add to Line Group

Partition   NewYork_PT

Directory Number Contains

Available DN/Route Partition   1001/NewYork_PT / 1002/NewYork_PT / 1003/NewYork_PT   Find

Add to Line Group

Current Line Group Members

Reverse Order of Selected DN/Route Partitions

Selected DN/Route Partition

Figure 6-2 Adding Line Group Members

Available DN/Route Partition   Find

Add to Line Group

Current Line Group Members

Reverse Order of Selected DN/Route Partitions

Selected DN/Route Partition   1003/NewYork_PT / 1001/NewYork_PT / 1002/NewYork_PT

Removed DN/Route Partition

Directory Numbers

Save   Delete   Add New

Figure 6-3 Move Directory Numbers Using Arrows

Configuring a Hunt List

1. Using a web browser, open https://10.0.1.20/ccmadmin, and enter the Application username and password.

2. Choose **Call Routing > Route/Hunt > Hunt List**. Click the **Add New** button.

3. Enter **Marketing_HL** as the name and **Marketing Hunt List** as the Description.

4. Select **CMGroup_2_1** as the Cisco Unified Communications Manager Group.

5. Check **Enable This Hunt List.**

6. Click **Save**, as shown in Figure 6-4.

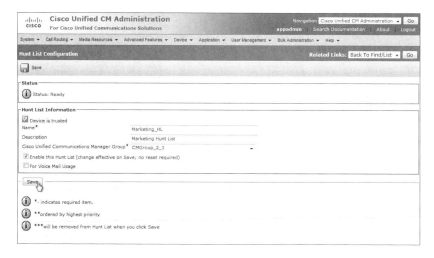

Figure 6-4   Configuring a Hunt List

7. After the save is successful, the Hunt List Member Information section appears. Click the **Add Line Group** button.

8. Choose the **Marketing_LG** Line Group, and click the **Save** button. (See Figure 6-5.)

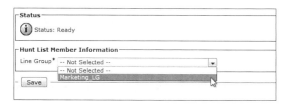

Figure 6-5   Choose Marketing_LG

9. Click the **Reset** button to enable the Line Group for the Hunt List.

Configuring a Hunt Pilot

The Hunt Pilot is the number that the caller uses to access the Hunt Group.

1. Using a web browser, open https://10.0.1.20/ccmadmin, and enter the Application username and password.

2. Choose **Call Routing > Route/Hunt > Hunt Pilot**. Click the **Add New** button.

3. Enter **1500** in the Hunt Pilot field. This field also accepts Route Pattern type strings for increased flexibility.

4. Select **NewYork_PT** as the Route Partition that can access this Hunt Pilot.

5. Enter **Marketing Hunt Pilot** as the Description.

6. Select **Marketing_HL** as the Hunt List.

7. Enter **Marketing** in the Alerting Name and ASCII Alerting Name fields.

8. Uncheck **Provide Outside Dial Tone.**

9. In the Hunt Forward Settings section, enter **4500**, which is the Directory Number chosen for Voicemail in this example. This setting enables CUCM to forward the call to voicemail when no DNs answer a call. (See Figure 6-6.)

10. Click **Save.**

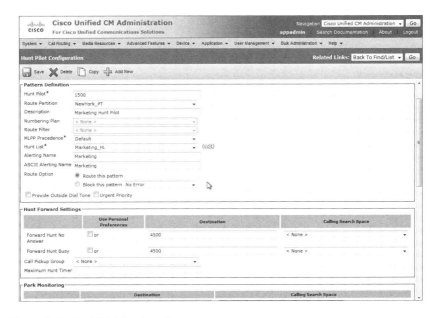

Figure 6-6 Hunt Pilot Configuration

Configuring Shared Lines

Shared Lines enables the ability to have more than one phone access the same Directory Number. This feature is often used by an administrative assistant to provide coverage for a department or a manager.

1. Using a web browser, open https://10.0.1.20/ccmadmin, and enter the Application username and password.

2. Choose **Device > Phone**, and click the **Find** button. A list of phones appears.

3. Click the link for the phone with the 1001 DN.

4. In the Association Information section on the left, click the link for **Line [2] – Add a New DN**. (See Figure 6-7.)

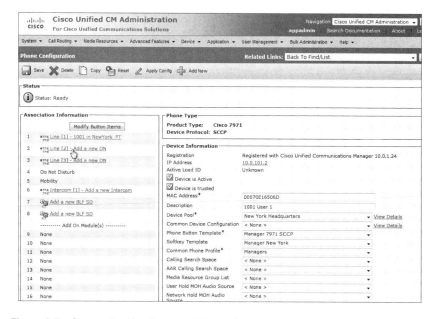

Figure 6-7   Choose the Line Button to Make a Shared Line

5. A new page appears. In the Directory Number field, enter **1003**.

6. Select **NewYork_PT** for the Route Partition. Because DN 1003 already exists in the system, the page automatically fetches the appropriate configuration for DN 1003, except for the **Line 2 on Device SEP<MAC ADDRESS>** section at the bottom of the page.

7. Scroll down to **Line 2 on Device SEP<MAC ADDRESS>**, and enter **Marketing User 3** in the Display (Internal Caller ID) field. Press the **Tab** key to move to the next field, and CUCM automatically fills it in for you.

8. Enter **1003 Marketing** in the Line Text Label field, and press the **Tab** key to auto-fill the ASCII Line Text Label field.

9. Click the **Save** button and then the **Apply Config** button.

10. In the Related Links navigation menu, select **Configure Device SEP<MAC ADDRESS>** and click the **Go** button.

You now see that Line 2 has DN 1003 as a shared line (see Figure 6-8).

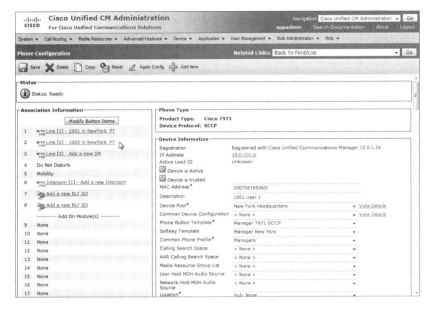

Figure 6-8   Verifying a Shared Line

Configuring Barge and Privacy

Barge enables users to conference into a call already in progress on one of the *shared lines* appearing on their phone. Privacy prevents the Barge feature from working and will not display the call information on phones that share the same DN.

First, verify that the relevant service parameters are set to allow Barge and Privacy, and then modify a button template to include a Barge and Privacy button. The following steps detail those tasks.

1. Using a web browser, open https://10.0.1.20/ccmadmin, and enter the Application username and password.

2. Choose **System > Service Parameters > 10.0.1.24 (Active) > Cisco CallManager (Active)**.

3. Scroll down to the **Clusterwide Parameters (Device – Phone)** section. For the **Builtin Bridge Enable**, select **On**. A message appears indicating that Barge cannot be used on 7960 and 7940 phones with encryption enabled. It also states that you must reset the phones for the configuration change to be active.

4. A little further down the page in the same Clusterwide Parameters (Device – Phone) section, make sure that the Privacy Setting is set to **True**. (See Figure 6-9.)

NOTE   If Privacy is set to True in the Clusterwide Parameters, barging will be blocked unless Privacy is set to **Off** in the Device Information settings for the phone. Configuring the settings in this manner enables only those whom you explicitly allow to use the barge feature.

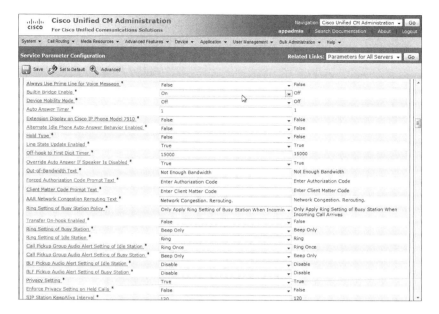

Figure 6-9   Make Sure the Privacy Setting Is Set to True

5. Scroll down to Clusterwide Parameters (Device – General) and verify that Party Entrance Tone is set to **True**. This setting tells the CUCM to play a tone when another party barges the call.

6. Further down the page, find the Clusterwide Parameters (Feature – Join Across Lines and Single Button Barge Feature Set) section. In the Single Button Barge/ CBarge Policy, select **Barge.**

7. Click **Save**.

8. Choose **Device > Device Settings > Softkey Template.**

9. Click the **Add New** button.

10. Select **Manager New York** to create a Softkey Template from. Click the **Copy** button.

11. Enter **Manager New York Barge** in the Name field, and click **Save.**

12. The page refreshes and a new menu option appears in the Related Links navigation menu. Select **Configure Softkey Layout.** (See Figure 6-10.)

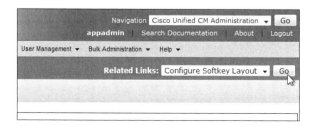

Figure 6-10   Softkey Template Configuration

13. In the **Softkey Layout Configuration** section, select **Remote In Use** from the Select a Call State to Configure menu.

14. Verify that **Barge** (Barge) is in the **Selected Softkeys** field. (See Figure 6-11.)

NOTE The word in parentheses is what displays on the phone's screen as the softkey label.

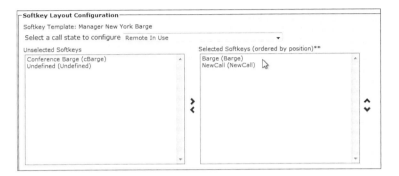

Figure 6-11   Verify the Barge is in the Selected Softkeys Field

15. Click **Save.**

16. Now, navigate to the device that should have the Barge feature, and apply the Softkey Template. See Chapter 5, "Cisco Unified Communications Manager (CUCM) Administration and Management," for steps to create and apply a Softkey Template.

17. To enable **Privacy**, add a Privacy button in the Phone Button Template, and apply the template to the phone. See Chapter 5 for steps to create and apply a Phone Button Template.

Configuring Call Forward

The Call Forward feature enables users to easily forward their calls to a destination of their choosing. The feature also gives the administrator control over the destinations allowed by using a restricted CSS. The following details the steps needed to configure the Call Forward feature.

In the headquarters, you want to restrict a user's ability to forward calls to the company operator. The same steps apply if you would like to restrict a user's ability to forward calls to other unapproved destinations.

1. Using a web browser, open https://10.0.1.20/ccmadmin, and enter the Application username and password.

2. Create a new **Partition** called **Blocked_PT**. See Chapter 5 for the steps needed to create Partitions.

3. Create a **Route Pattern** of **0** with the settings indicated in Figure 6-12. See Chapter 5 for more details on creating Route Patterns.

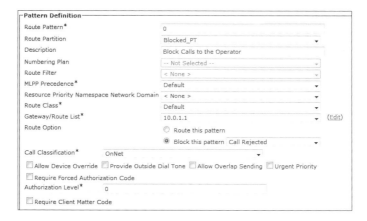

Figure 6-12   Create a Route Pattern of 0

4. Create a new **Calling Search Space** using the setting specified in Figure 6-13. Be sure that the **Selected Partitions** field contains **Blocked_PT.** In this example, you allow calls to be forwarded to internal four-digit numbers and blocking calls to routes using Blocked_PT. See Chapter 5 for more details on creating Calling Search Spaces.

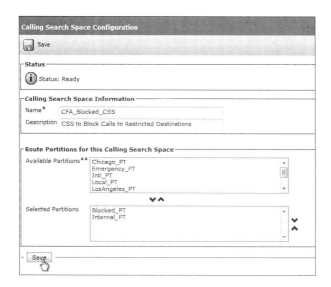

Figure 6-13   Save the Selected Partitions

5. Create a Softkey Template that includes the Forward All (CfwdAll) softkey in the On Hook and Off Hook states. (See Figure 6-14.) Apply that Softkey Template to the appropriate phone.

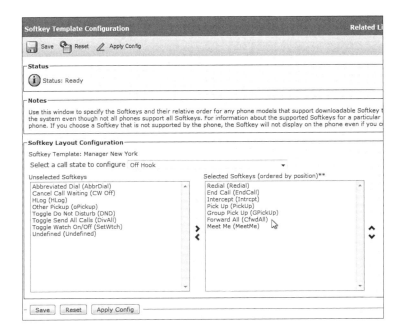

Figure 6-14   Create Softkey Template with CfwdAll

6. Choose **Device > Phone** and click the **Find** button.

7. Choose the phone you want to apply the CFA_Blocked_CSS Calling Search Space to.

8. Choose Line 1 on the phone, and scroll down to the Call Forward and Call Pickup Settings section.

9. In the Forward All Calling Search Space column, select **CFA_Blocked_CSS**. (See Figure 6-15.)

10. Click the **Save** button and then the **Apply Config** button.

NOTE   If the user presses the **CfwdAll** softkey and then presses **0**, the CUCM plays the reorder tone. If the user tried to forward to either voicemail or some other internal number, the CUCM would allow the forwarding to proceed.

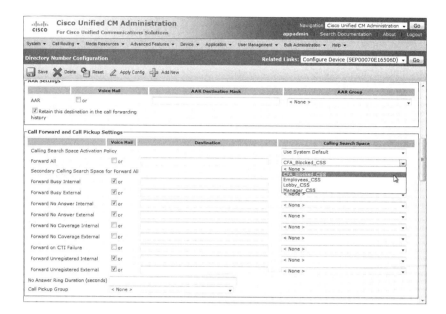

Figure 6-15   Apply CFA_Blocked_CSS to Forward All Setting

Configuring Call Pickup

The Call Pickup feature enables the user to answer calls ringing on other phones remotely. You configure a Marketing Pickup Group so that any available marketing personnel can answer any ringing phone from their own desk.

1. Using a web browser, open https://10.0.1.20/ccmadmin, and enter the Application username and password.

2. Choose **Call Routing > Call Pickup Group**.

3. Click the **Add New** button.

4. Enter **Marketing_PG** as the Call Pickup Group Name.

5. Enter **8005** as the Call Pickup Group Number.

6. Enter **Marketing Pickup Group** as the Description.

7. Select **Internal_PT** as the Partition so that only phones assigned to the Internal Partition can access the pickup group.

8. Select **Audio and Visual Alert** as the Call Pickup Group Notification Policy. (See Figure 6-16.)

9. Click the **Save** button.

10. Now assign the Pickup Group to a device. Choose **Device > Phone**, and click the **Find** button.

11. Click the **SEP<MACADDRESS>** link for **1002 User 2**. (See Figure 6-17.)

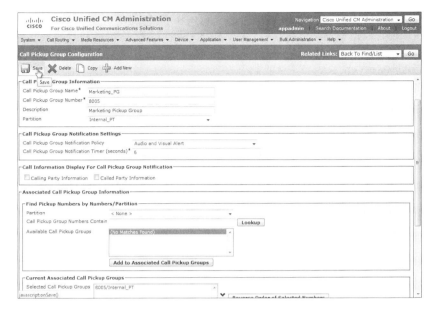

Figure 6-16 Call Pickup Group Settings

Figure 6-17 Choose a Device to Make a Member of the Pickup Group

12. Click the link for **Line [1] – 1002 in NewYork_PT**.

13. Scroll down to the Call Forward and Call Pickup Settings section.

14. At the bottom of the section, select **Marketing_PG in Internal_PT** as the Call Pickup Group. (See Figure 6-18.)

15. Click **Save** and **Apply Config**.

16. Add other phones to the Pickup Group the same way.

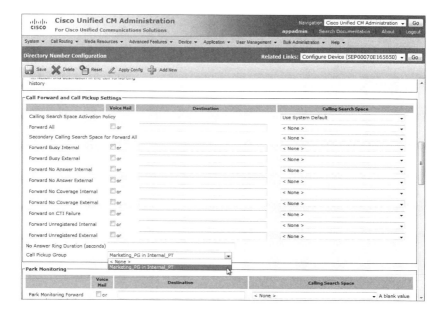

Figure 6-18   Select the Call Pickup Group

Configuring Call Park

The Call Park feature enables a user to place a call on hold and then have the call picked up by any other phone by dialing a number assigned to the held call. This feature is useful in businesses like a warehouse, car dealership, factory, or large store where there are general-use phones in various locations. A user hears a page, "Mike, a Call Holding for You on 7001." Mike chooses the nearest phone and dials 7001 and is connected to the held call.

In this scenario, CUCM dynamically assigns a Call Park number from a range, 7001 to 7009, and parks the call there. The number that the call is parked at displays on the screen for approximately 10 seconds.

1. Using a web browser, open https://10.0.1.20/ccmadmin, and enter the Application username and password.

2. Choose **Call Routing > Call Park**, and click the **Add New** button.

3. Enter **700[1-9]** as the Call Park Number/Range.

4. Enter **Call Park 7001 – 7009** as the Description.

5. Select **Internal_PT** as the Partition.

6. Choose **subscriber** as the Cisco Unified Communications Manager. (See Figure 6-19.)

> **TIP**   If you want to assign Call Park numbers or ranges to more than one subscriber, be sure to use different numbers or ranges for each subscriber.

Figure 6-19   Call Park Configuration

7. Click the **Save** button.

8. Now you need to make sure that the devices you want to use the Call Park feature have the **Park** softkey assigned in the Connected state. See Chapter 5 for details about how to modify and apply Softkey Templates.

Configuring Directed Call Park

The Directed Call Park differs from the Call Park feature in that the user placing the call in Park decides what DN to use to park the call. This is useful where Marketing might have one range of numbers for parked calls and Sales might have another range of numbers. It is basically a way to allow the users to have more control over how to park calls.

In this scenario, a user hears "Call holding on Line 7010." Because people at that site know that the Marketing department's calls are parked at 701<*some number from 0 to 9*>, everyone except those in the Marketing department ignore the announcement. Someone from Marketing goes to any available phone and dials ***77010** to retrieve the parked call.

1. Using a web browser, open https://10.0.1.20/ccmadmin, and enter the Application username and password.

2. Choose **Call Routing > Directed Call Park**, and click the **Add New** button.

3. Enter **701X** as the Call Park Number/Range.

4. Enter **Marketing Call Park Range** as the Description.

5. Select **Internal_PT** as the Partition.

6. Enter **1005** for the reversion number so that any calls not picked up ring back to the assistant at DN 1005.

7. Select **Employees_CSS** as the Reversion Calling Search Space.

8. Enter ***7** as the Retrieval Prefix. This prefix must be dialed by the person trying to retrieve the parked call. To retrieve a call parked at 7010, she would dial ***77010**.

9. Click the **Save** button. (See Figure 6-20.)

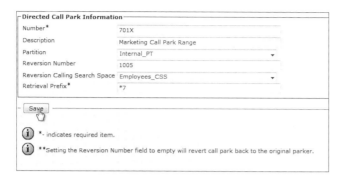

Figure 6-20   Directed Call Park Configuration

NOTE   To use the Directed Call Park feature, the person parking the call must press the Transfer button and transfer the call to a number in the range, in this case 7010.

Configuring Native Presence (Busy Lamp Field [BLF] Speed Dial)

The Busy Lamp Field (BLF) Speed Dial is CUCM's native presence feature. By configuring BLF buttons on a correctly configured device, the user can view the On-hook and Off-hook states of a DN. The following details the steps needed to configure BLF buttons.

NOTE   The BLF buttons cannot be a softkey, so the device you want to configure the BLF button on must have available Line buttons.

1. Using a web browser, open https://10.0.1.20/ccmadmin, and enter the Application username and password.

2. Choose **Device > Device Settings > Phone Button Template**, and configure a Phone Button Template. **Add 3 Speed Dial BLF Features** to it. See Chapter 5 for details on how to create and apply a Phone Button Template.

3. Choose **Device > Phone** and click the **Find** button. Click the **SEP<MACADDRESS>** link for **1002 User 2.**

4. Select the new Phone Button Template **Standard 7971 SCCP with 3 BLF**; click **Save** and **Apply Config.** (See Figure 6-21.)

5. In the Association Information section, click the link for **Add a new BLF SD**. (See Figure 6-22.)

6. A new window appears. In the Busy Lamp Field/Speed Dial Button Settings section, the second column is labeled Directory Number. Select **1001 in NewYork_PT** from the drop-down list.

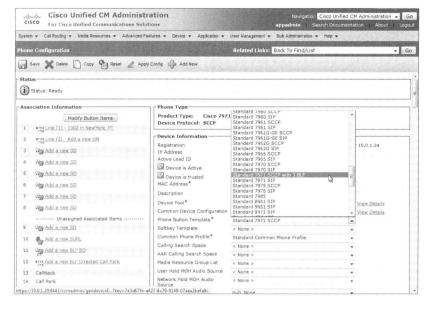

Figure 6-21   Select Phone Button Template with BLF

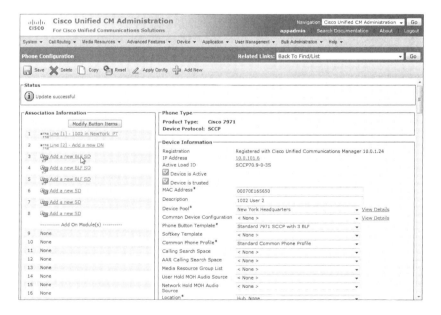

Figure 6-22   Choose BLF_SD to Configure

TIP   You can assign all BLF buttons from this window. There is no need to configure each one by clicking the link in the Association Information section.

7. Select **1003 in NewYork_PT** as the second BLF. (See Figure 6-23.)

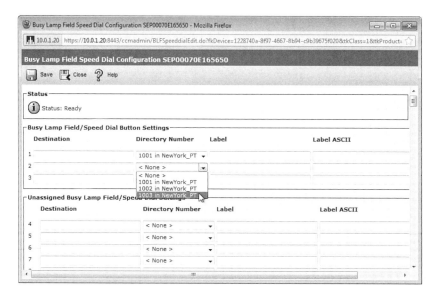

Figure 6-23   Select the DN for the BLF Speed Dial

8. Click **Save** and then **Close**. The BLF Speed Dials are now listed in the
    Association Information section. (See Figure 6-24.)

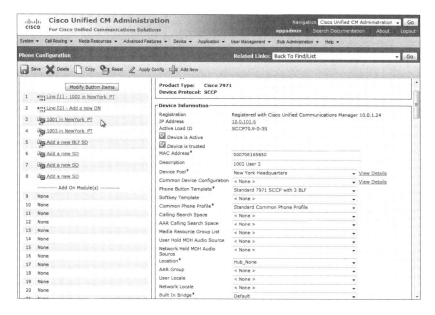

Figure 6-24   BLF Configuration Example

9. In the Protocol Specific Information section, select **Employees_CSS** as the SUBSCRIBE Calling Search Space.

10. Click **Save** and **Apply Config**.

Configuring Extension Mobility

The Extension Mobility feature enables users to sit at any available desk and log in to the phone. When logged in, the phone refreshes with all the user's speed dials and settings. This feature is useful in offices where the desks are unassigned or shared.

1. Verify that the Cisco Extension Mobility service is activated by using a web browser to open https://10.0.1.20/ccmservice, and enter the Application username and password.

2. Choose **Tools > Service Activation**. Select **10.0.1.24** (the Subscriber). Verify that **Cisco Extension Mobility** is checked and activated. If it is not activated, activate it at this time. See Chapter 5 for more information about activating services.

3. Using the main Navigation menu in the upper-right corner, select **Cisco Unified CM Administration** and click the **Go** button.

4. Choose **System > Service Parameters > 10.0.1.24 (Active) > Cisco Extension Mobility (Active)**.

5. Select **Auto Logout** for the Intra-cluster Multiple Login Behavior field because you want to make it easier on your users to log in to whichever device they choose regardless of whether they are currently logged in elsewhere.

6. Select **False** for the Alphanumeric User ID field because your users all have numeric user IDs.

7. Click the **Save** button.

8. Choose **Device > Device Settings > Phone Services**. Click **Add New.**

9. Enter **Extension Mobility** in the Service Name field. Click in the ASCII Service Name field, and the field will be automatically filled for you.

10. Enter **http://10.0.1.20:8080/emapp/EMAppServlet?device=#DEVICENAME#** in the Service URL field.

NOTE The preceding service URL is case sensitive and does not work if entered incorrectly.

11. Check the **Enable** box. Leave the Enterprise Subscription box unchecked.

12. Click **Save**. (See Figure 6-25.)

13. Now configure the Device Profile that controls how the phone behaves when it is not logged into. This basically configures the phone in its default state with no user associated to it, so you need to assign a DN, Partition, and Calling Search Space.

14. Choose **Device > Device Settings > Device Profile**, and click the **Add New** button.

Figure 6-25   IP Phone Services Configuration

15. Select **Cisco 7971** as the Device Profile Type. Click the **Next** button.

16. Select **SCCP** as the Device Protocol, and click the **Next** button.

17. Enter **7971_LoggedOut_EM** in the Device Profile Name field, and enter **7971 with Extension Mobility Logged Out Profile** in the Description field.

18. Select **Standard 7971 SCCP** as the Phone Button Template, and click the **Save** button. (See Figure 6-26.)

Figure 6-26   Select the Phone Button Template

19. The page refreshes and adds the Association Info section.

20. Click the link for **Line [1] – Add a New DN.**

21. Enter the following from Table 6-3 in the appropriate fields. See Chapter 5 for more details on adding a new DN. This device is configured to allow only internal (and 911) calls. Click the **Save** button when done.

Table 6-3   Device Profile Configuration Information for Extension Mobility

Directory Number	1010
Route Partition	Internal_PT
Description	Shared Desk
Alerting Name	Shared Desk
ASCII Alerting Name	Shared Desk
Calling Search Space	Lobby_CSS
Forward All CSS	CFA_Blocked_CSS
Display (Internal Caller ID)	Shared Desk
ASCII Display (Internal Caller ID)	Shared Desk

22. From the Related Links menu, select **Configure Device (7971_with_EM)** and click the **Go** button.

23. From the Related Links menu, select **Subscribe/Unsubscribe Services**, and click the **Go** button.

24. Select **Extension Mobility** from the Select a Service drop-down, and click **Next.**

25. Leave the Service Name and ASCII Service Name as **Extension Mobility**, and click the **Subscribe** button.

26. Click the **Save** button and close the window. (See Figure 6-27.)

27. Click the **Save** button on the Device Profile Configuration window.

28. Now define a profile for a user that can use the Extension Mobility service. Click the **Copy** button.

29. Use Table 6-4 to create the profile, and click **Save**. (See Figure 6-28.)

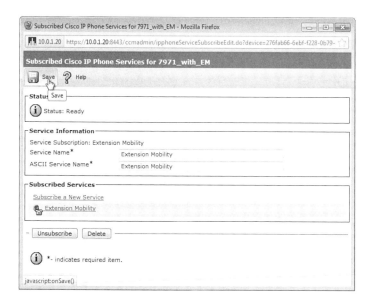

Figure 6-27   Subscribed Service Name Configuration

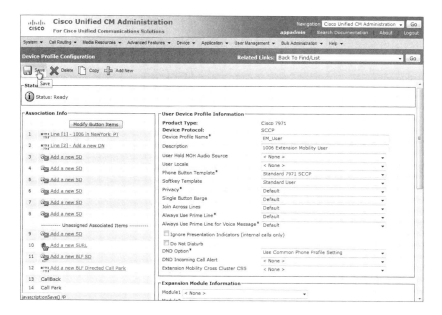

Figure 6-28   Click Save for the Extension Mobility Device Profile

Table 6-4   User Device Profile Information

Device Profile Name	EM_User
Description	1006 Extension Mobility User
Softkey Template	Standard User
Directory Number	1006
Route Partition	NewYork_PT
Description	1006 User 6
Alerting Name	1006 User 6
ASCII Alerting Name	1006 User 6
Calling Search Space	Employees_CSS
Forward All CSS	CFA_Blocked_CSS
Display (Internal Caller ID)	1006 User 6
ASCII Display (Internal Caller ID)	1006 User 6

WARNING   Be sure to subscribe to the Extension Mobility service in the User Device Profile. The users cannot log out if you don't subscribe their Device Profile to the Extension Mobility Service.

30.   Create a new end user with a user ID of **1006**. See Chapter 5 for the steps needed to create a user.

31.   In the Extension Mobility section, move **EM_User** from the Available Profiles field to the Controlled Profiles Field. (See Figure 6-29.)

Figure 6-29   Move EM_User to Controlled Profiles Using Arrows Between Boxes

32. Click the **Save** button.

33. Now modify a device to enable Extension Mobility, and apply a Log Out Profile on the device.

34. Choose **Device > Phone** and click the **Find** button.

35. Click the **SEP<MACADDRESS>** link for **1001 User 1.** Turn this phone into an Extension Mobility Phone.

36. Scroll down to the **Extension Information** section, and Check **Enable Extension Mobility**.

37. Select **7971_LoggedOut_EM** as the Log Out Profile. (See Figure 6-30.)

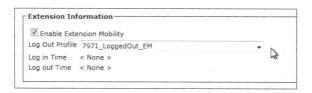

Figure 6-30   Enabling Extension Mobility

38. Click the **Save** button and then the **Apply Config** button.

39. A user can now press the **Services** button on the phone that formerly had DN 1001 on line 1 and log in with the user ID **1006** and PIN set in Step 30.

Configuring Intercom

The Intercom feature enables a caller to initiate a one-way audio Whisper to a recipient without having to ring a phone. The first party simply presses a button or dials a configured intercom number or DN and is immediately connected to the receiving device and can begin speaking. If the receiver wants to speak with the initiator, the receiver needs to press the mute button to unmute the calling party or dial a number to establish a voice path back to the initiator. The following steps detail how to configure the Intercom feature.

NOTE   Intercom uses its own dial plan, separate from the rest of the system. As such, you can create duplicates of DNs that you already have in place, or use fewer digits to make using the intercom easier. In this example, you use two digits as your Intercom DN. If the Intercom feature were integrated in the rest of the dial plan and a user dialed two digits, the system would wait for more digits to be entered until the interdigit timeout expires. That is just one reason that it is convenient that Intercom uses its own dial plan/numbering scheme.

1. Using a web browser, open https://10.0.1.20/ccmadmin, and enter the Application username and password.

2. Choose **Call Routing > Intercom > Intercom Route Partition.** Click the **Add New** button.

3. Enter **Marketing_IC, Marketing Intercom** in the Name field. Click **Save.**

4. Choose **Call Routing > Intercom > Intercom Calling Search Space**, and verify that **Marketing_IC_GEN** was automatically created.

5. Choose **Call Routing > Intercom > Intercom Directory Number**. Click the **Add New** button.

6. Enter **70** to **71** in the Intercom Directory Number field. Always enter Intercom numbers in pairs.

7. Select **Marketing_IC** as the Route Partition.

8. Enter **Marketing Intercom** in the Description, Alerting Name, and ASCII Alerting Name fields.

9. Select **Marketing_IC_GEN** as the Calling Search Space, and click the **Save** button. (See Figure 6-31.)

Figure 6-31   Configuring Intercom DN

10. The page refreshes and shows the last Intercom DN that was configured. From the Related Links menu, select **Back to Find/List** and click the **Go** button. You can verify that both Intercom Directory Numbers were created.

11. Now add an Intercom button to a Phone Button Template. Modify **Standard 7971 SCCP with 3 BLF** created earlier and change row 6 from Speed Dial to **Intercom**. See Chapter 5 for details on how to modify a Phone Button Template. Be sure to click the **Apply Config** button so that the new template is applied to the phones.

12. Now add the Intercom DN to the appropriate devices. Choose **Device > Phone**, and click the **Find** button. Assign Intercom DN 70 to 1001 User 1 and Intercom DN 71 to 1002 User 2. Click the **SEP<MACADDRESS>** link for **1001 User 1**.

13. Click the link for **Intercom [1] – Add a New Intercom** in the Association Information section. (See Figure 6-32.)

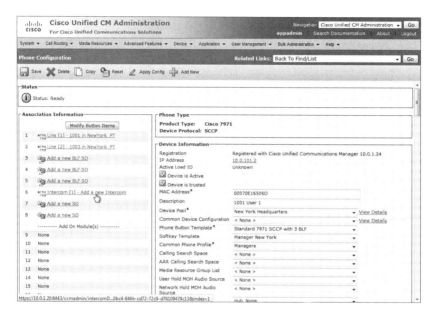

Figure 6-32   Choose a Button for the Intercom Feature

14. Enter **70** in the Intercom Directory Number field. After the page refreshes, the correct CSS and other information are automatically prefilled for you.

15. For the Default Activated Device field, select the **SEP<MACADDRESS>** for the device that you want the Intercom button to appear on. If you don't make a selection here, the Intercom button does not appear on the phone.

16. Enter **User 1** in the Display (Internal Caller ID) field. The ASCII Display (Internal Caller ID) is automatically filled. Enter **Intercom** as the Line Text Label, and the ASCII Line Text Label is automatically filled.

17. Enter **71** in the Speed Dial field. Entering the receiving party's Intercom DN here allows the caller to press the Intercom button and not need to dial a number to reach the intended party. Click the **Save** button.

18. Repeat the steps for 1002 User 2 using Intercom DN 71 and Speed Dial 70. Click **Save** and **Apply Config**. (See Figure 6-33.)

Figure 6-33   Configuring the Intercom on the Button

Configuring Mobile Connect

The Mobile Connect feature is the Single Number Reach feature that enables the user to use a cell phone with a desk phone by extending calls to the cellular network from the CUCM.

1. Using a web browser, open https://10.0.1.20/ccmadmin, and enter the Application username and password.

2. Modify the **Manager New York** Softkey Template to include the **Mobility** softkey in both the On Hook and Connected call states. See Chapter 5 for details on how to configure a Softkey Template.

3. Choose **User Management > End User**, and click user ID **1001**.

4. Scroll down to the Mobility Information section, and check the **Enable Mobility** box. Select **SEP00070E16506D** from the Primary User Device drop-down. Click the **Save** button. (See Figure 6-34.)

5. Choose **Device > Phone** and click the **Find** button.

6. Click the **SEP<MACADDRESS>** link for **1001 User 1**, and select **1001** for the Owner User ID field. (See Figure 6-35.)

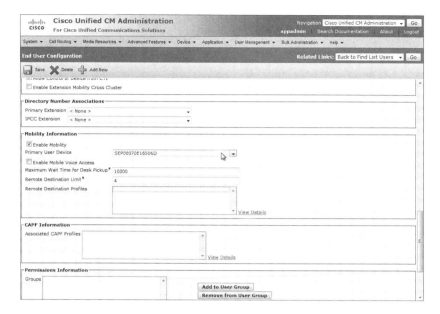

Figure 6-34   Check to Enable Mobility

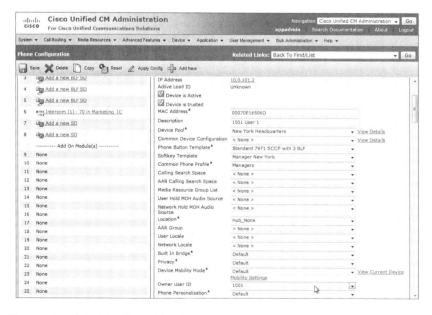

Figure 6-35   Select the Owner User ID

7. Choose **Device > Device Settings > Remote Destination Profile.** Click the **Add New** button.

8. Enter **NY_Marketing_Manager_RD** in the Name field and **Marketing Manager Remote Destination** in the Description field.

9. Select **1001** in the User ID field. Select **New York Headquarters** for the Device Pool field and **Manager_CSS** for both the Calling Search Space and Rerouting Calling Search Space fields. (See Figure 6-36.)

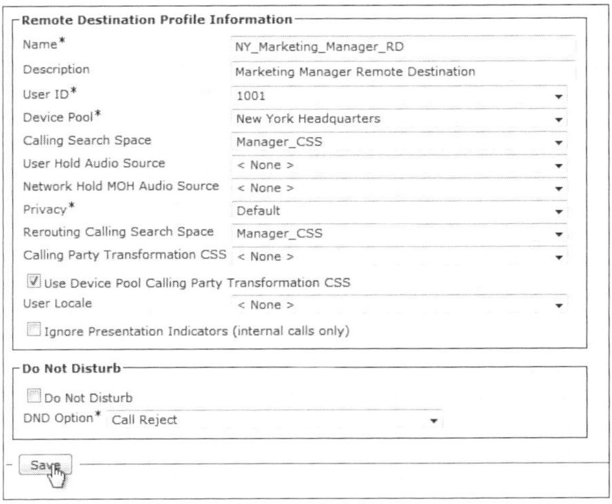

Figure 6-36   Configure the Remote Destination Profile

10. Click the **Save** button, and the page refreshes adding an Associated Remote Destinations section and an Association Information column with Line [1] – Add a New DN.

11. Click the link to **Add a New Remote Destination**. This is where you assign the cell phone number and schedule to ring the cell phone because the manager probably doesn't want to be disturbed on the weekends or after 6 p.m. on the weekdays.

12. Enter **Manager's Cell Phone** in the Name Field, and enter **92125551234** in the Destination Number field.

NOTE   Enter the number in the Destination Number field as if it were dialed from a phone on the system. If your site has an access code, such as 9, then you would need to include that as well.

13. Check the boxes for **Mobile Phone** and **Enable Mobile Connect**.

14. In the Ring Schedule section, check the box next to the day and enter the hours, in 24-hour time format, that the manager would like to have in his cell phone ring, **09:00 to 18:00 Monday Through Friday**. **No hours on the Weekend**. Be sure to choose the correct time zone, in this case (**GMT -5:00) America/New_York**. (See Figure 6-37.)

Figure 6-37   Configure the Ring Schedule

15. Because the marketing manager doesn't want every call to ring his cell phone, you need to create an access list to allow only certain numbers to ring the cell phone. Create an allowed number list by navigating to **Call Routing > Class of Control > Access List**. Click the **Add New** button.

16. Now configure an allow list that includes the marketing manager's spouse and any four-digit number. Enter **Marketing_Allow** in the Name field and **Marketing Manager's Allow List** in the Description field. Select **1001** from the Owner drop-down menu, and select the **Allowed** radio button. Click the **Save** button. (See Figure 6-38.)

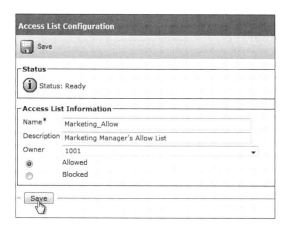

Figure 6-38   Save the Access List

17. The page refreshes and a new section appears. In the Access List Member section, click the **Add Member** button. Leave **Directory Number** in the Filter Mask field. In the DN Mask field, enter **2125554567** because this is the ANI (Caller ID) of the manager's spouse. Click the **Save** button and then repeat for four-digit numbers. Use **XXXX** as the DN Mask field. Click the **Save** button. (See Figure 6-39.)

Figure 6-39   Add Allowed Numbers

18. Now apply the access list to the Remote Destination by choosing **Device > Remote Destination.** Click the **Find** button, and then click the link for **Manager's Cell Phone.**

19. Scroll down to the When Receiving a Call During the Above Ring Schedule section and click the radio button next to **Ring This Destination Only if Caller Is In** and then select **Marketing_Allow.** Click the **Save** button. (See Figure 6-40.)

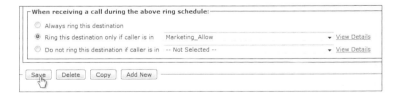

Figure 6-40   Select the Marketing_Allow Access List

Configuring Mobile Voice Access (MVA)

The Mobile Voice Access feature enables a user to call into a special number and place calls as if the calls were originated from the user's IP Phone.

1. Verify that the Mobile Voice Access service is activated. Using a web browser, open https://10.0.1.20/ccmservice and enter the Application username and password.

2. Choose **Tools > Service Activation**. Select **10.0.1.20** (the Publisher) and verify that the check box next to **Cisco Unified Mobile Voice Access Service** is checked. (See Figure 6-41.) Use the main navigation drop-down on the upper right to select **Cisco Unified CM Administration**, and click the **Go** button.

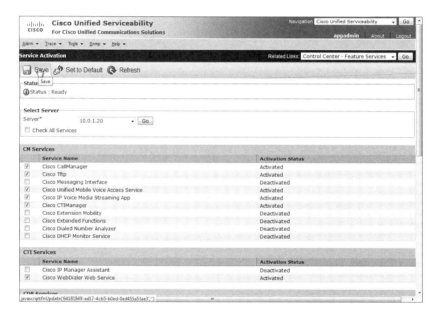

Figure 6-41   Enable the Cisco Unified Mobile Voice Access Service

3. Choose **System > Service Parameters > 10.0.1.20 (Active) > Cisco CallManager (Active)**.

4. Scroll down to almost the end of the page to Clusterwide Parameters (System-Mobility). Select **True** for the Enable Mobile Voice Access field.

5. Select **True** for the Enable Enterprise Feature Access field so that users can place a call on hold or transfer a call using codes preceded by an asterisk (that is,***81** for Hold). The codes are also located in the Clusterwide Parameters (System-Mobility) section for your reference.

6. Enter **5500** as the Mobile Voice Access number that users dial to use the Mobility feature. It should be a Direct Inward Dial (DID) number that users can reach directly from outside of your organization.

7. Enter **9911, 911** in the System Remote Access Blocked Numbers field so that 911
    cannot be dialed using Mobile Voice Access because emergency services could
    get an incorrect address.

8. Click the **Save** button. (See Figure 6-42.)

Figure 6-42   Configure Service Parameters for Mobility

9. Now enable the user for Mobile Voice Access. Choose **User Management > End
    User.** Select user ID **1001**.

10. In the Mobility Information section, check the box next to **Enable Mobile Voice
    Access.** Click the **Save** button. (See Figure 6-43.)

Figure 6-43   Enable Mobility for a User ID

11. Now configure the Mobile Voice Access Media Resource by choosing **Media
    Resources > Mobile Voice Access.**

12. Enter **5500** for the Mobile Voice Access Directory number, and select
NewYork_PT as the Mobile Voice Access Partition. Move **English United
States** down to the Selected Locales field, and click the **Save** button. (See Figure
6-44.)

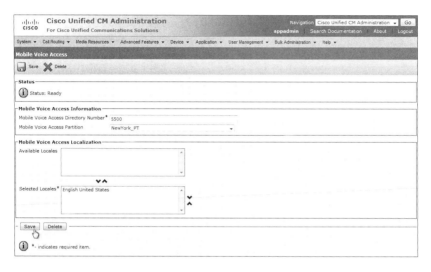

Figure 6-44   Configure the Mobile Voice Access DN and Partition

13. Configure the IOS Gateway with the VXML Application for Mobile Voice
Access and create dial peers.

NewYork(config)#**application**	Defines application.
NewYork(config-app)#**service** MobileVoiceAccess http://10.0.1.20:8080/ccmivr/ pages/IVRMainpage.vxml	Defines URL for the service named MobileVoiceAccess.
NewYork(config-app)#**exit**	Exits application configuration mode.
NewYork(config)#**dial-peer voice** **2125555500 pots**	Creates POTS dial peer with ID 2125555500.
NewYork(config-dial- peer)#**service MobileVoiceAccess**	Associates the service MobileVoiceAccess with this dial peer.
NewYork(config-dial- peer)#**incoming called-number** **2125555500**	Uses this dial peer if 2125555500 is the number that was called.
NewYork(config-dial- peer)#**direct-inward-dial**	Instructs the gateway to directly match 2125555500 to an outbound dial peer.
NewYork(config-dial-peer)#**exit**	Exits dial peer configuration.
NewYork(config)#**dial-peer voice** **5555500 voip**	Creates VoIP dial peer with ID 5555500.

NewYork(config-dial-peer)#**destination-pattern 2125555500**	Use this dial peer if matched from an inbound dial peer.
NewYork(config-dial-peer)#**session target ipv4:10.0.1.20**	Send the call to the CUCM.
NewYork(config-dial-peer)#**dtmf-relay h245-alphanumeric**	Enables relay of DTMF tones.
NewYork(config-dial-peer)#**codec G711Ulaw**	Use high-quality G711 codec.
NewYork(config-dial-peer)#**no vad**	Disables Voice Activity Detection enabling toll quality calls.
NewYork(config-dial-peer)#**exit**	Exits dial peer configuration.
NewYork(config)#**exit**	Exits global configuration mode.

```
dial-peer voice 2125555500 pots
 service mobilevoiceaccess
 incoming called-number 2125555500
 direct-inward-dial
!
dial-peer voice 5555500 voip
 destination-pattern 2125555500
 session target ipv4:10.0.1.20
 dtmf-relay h245-alphanumeric
 codec g711ulaw
 no vad
```

Summary

Using the steps outlined in this chapter, you can configure the most commonly used features in CUCM. Although CUCM offers many more features and configuration options, the steps detailed here typically suffice for most user populations.

CHAPTER 7

Cisco Unity Connection and Cisco Unified Presence

This chapter provides information and commands concerning the following topics:

- Cisco Unity Connection Administration Interfaces
- Configuring Class of Service in Cisco Unity Connection
- Configuring Partitions and Search Spaces in Unity Connection
- Configuring User Templates in Cisco Unity Connection
- Managing Users in Cisco Unity Connection
  - Adding users manually
  - Importing users via AXL from CUCM
  - Importing users with LDAP
  - Importing users with BAT
- Configuring Call Handlers in Cisco Unity Connection
- Cisco Unity Connection Reports
- Cisco Unified Presence Server Administration Interfaces
- Cisco Unity Connection and Cisco Unified Presence Backup and Restore

Topology

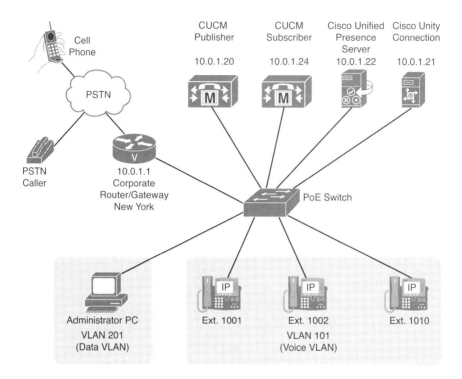

Figure 7-1   Topology

Cisco Unity Connection Administration Interfaces

Cisco Unity Connection

There are six administration interfaces for Cisco Unity Connection. Five interfaces are available via web-based GUI and one CLI available via SSH. It might be confusing to remember which login to use for a particular administration interface.

To help you avoid the confusion, Table 7-1 lists the name of the administration interface, the method to access the interface, and what username and password to use.

If you have more than one Cisco Unity Connection server in a cluster, be sure to perform all administration on the first node (Publisher).

Table 7-1 Cisco Unity Connection Administration Interfaces

Administration Interface	Access Method	Username/Password Combo
Cisco Unity Connection Administration	https://<IPAddress>/cuadmin	Application Username/Password
Cisco Unified Serviceability	https://<IPAddress>/ccmservice	Application Username/Password
Cisco Unified OS Administration	https://<IPAddress>/cmplatform	Platform Username/Password
Disaster Recovery System	https://<IPAddress>/drf	Platform Username/Password
Cisco Unity Connection Serviceability	https://<IPAddress>/cuservice	Application Username/Password
Command Line Interface	SSH to <IPAddress>	Platform Username/Password
NOTE There is a web interface for end users to access their voice messages and manage their account. Their account must have a Class of Service (COS) that enables access to the Cisco Personal Communications Assistant (PCA)		
End User Web Access	https://<IPAddress>/ciscopca	End UserID / Password

TIP You can also access the various web GUIs by using the drop-down menu in the upper-right corner of the web page and then clicking the **Go** button.

NOTE You can switch between interfaces using the same username/password combo without logging in each time. For example, if you were already logged in to the Cisco Unified Serviceability interface and switched to the Cisco Unity Connection Administration interface, you would not need to log in again because they use the same username and password.

Table 7-2 Common CLI Commands

admin:?	Shows available commands
admin:help <command>	Help for a command.
admin:show version active	Displays active system version.
admin:show version inactive	Displays if there are any other alternative versions installed. This is used when an upgrade is performed.
admin:utils service list	Displays a list of services and their status.
admin:show tech all	Displays useful information for Cisco TAC.
admin:utils network ping <IPAddress>	Pings an address and displays the result.

`admin:utils network traceroute <IPAddress>`	Performs a traceroute to an IP address and displays the result.
`admin:quit`	Logs you out and ends the management session.

TIP   You can press the **Tab** key to autocomplete some commands. You can also press the **up-arrow key** to recall previously entered commands.

NOTE   Complete words must be entered when issuing commands. A command such as **sh tech sys hardware** does not work because it does not use the complete words.

CAUTION   Be careful when using the CLI. Some commands that can affect system stability have Are You Sure prompts, but not all. Take the time to research commands and be familiar with the effects before pressing the **Enter** key.

Configuring Class of Service in Cisco Unity Connection

This section refers to the network topology referred to in Figure 7-1 and provides configuration steps for Class of Service (COS) in Unity Connection.

The COS defines what features and permissions a user has access to. It also defines the maximum length of the recorded name, greeting, and message.

NOTE   The web management interface differs in some ways from the CUCM because the menu items display along the side of the page vertically instead of along the top of the page horizontally. (See Figure 7-2.) Some similarities include the Navigation menu in the upper right with the **Go** button and that you must save your changes on the page before leaving or the changes would be lost.

1. Using a web browser, open https://10.0.1.21/cuadmin, and enter the Application username and password.

2. Choose **Class of Service > Class of Service**. Click the **Add New** button. (Refer to Figure 7-2.)

3. Enter **Employees_NY_COS** as the Display Name.

4. Under Licensed Features, check **Allow Users to Access Voice Mail Using an IMAP Client**. This allows users to use an IMAP email client to access messages for easier message management.

5. Under Features, check **Allow Users to Use the Messaging Assistant**. This feature enables the user to access the Cisco Personal Communications Assistant (PCA), which is a web interface for users to manage their messages.

6. Under Message Options, uncheck **Allow Users to Send Messages to System Distribution Lists** because this option could be abused. (See Figure 7-3.)

7. Click the **Save** button.

Figure 7-2   Adding a COS

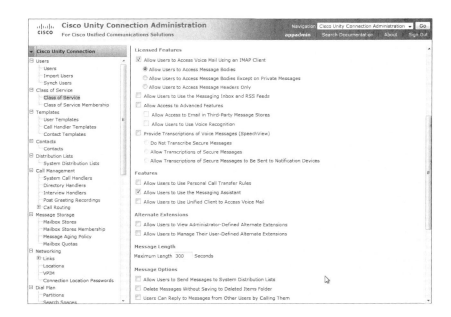

Figure 7-3   Restricting Access to System Distribution Lists

Configuring Partitions and Search Spaces in Unity Connection

Partitions and Search Spaces serve a similar function in Cisco Unity Connection as they do in CUCM. Partitions are logical groupings of devices with similar reachability, and a Search Space is an ordered list of partitions.

Extensions must be unique within a Partition, but in a Search Space they do not need to be. So you can have overlapping extensions in a Search Space, like 0 (zero).

In Figure 7-4 the Partitions are organized at the top indicating three locations. Below the Partitions are the Search Spaces that contain an ordered list of Partitions for reachability. The Executives_SS Search Space can access NewYork_PT, Chicago_PT, and LosAngeles_PT, making it possible to do things like send a companywide broadcast message and perform directory searches. The Employees_SS for each location have access to only their own location, and the Marketing_SS Search Space has access to both NewYork_PT and LosAngeles_PT because there are Marketing teams in both locations.

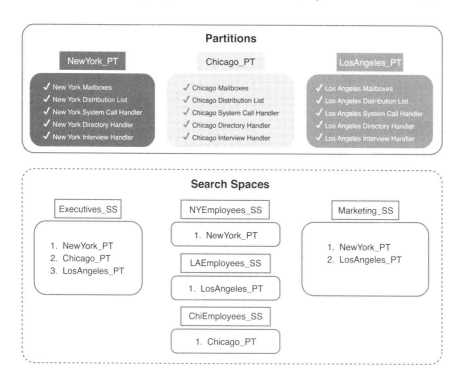

Figure 7-4   Partition and Calling Search Space Relationships

When you are designing your dial plan, it is a good idea to logically separate the areas if possible so that features and functions, like Handlers and Directories, are sectioned from one another, increasing flexibility and lessening the chance for system conflict by overlapping numbers.

To configure a Partition, follow these steps:

1. Using a web browser, open https://10.0.1.21/cuadmin, and enter the Application username and password.

2. Choose **Dial Plan > Partitions**. Click the **Add New** button.

3. Enter **NewYork_PT** in the Name field, and click the **Save** button.

4. The page refreshes, and you can now enter **New York Employees** in the Description field; click the **Save** button.

To configure a Search Space, follow these steps:

1. Using a web browser, open https://10.0.1.21/cuadmin, and enter the Application username and password.

2. Choose **Dial Plan > Search Spaces**. Click the **Add New** button.

3. Enter **Executives_SS** in the Name field, and click the **Save** button.

4. The page refreshes, and you can now enter **New York Employees** in the Description field; click the **Save** button.

5. Move the Partitions from the Unassigned Partitions field up to the Assigned Partitions field by selecting the Partition you want to move and then using the up arrow between the fields. You can then rearrange the order of the Partitions in the Assigned Partitions field using the arrows on the side of the field. (See Figure 7-5.)

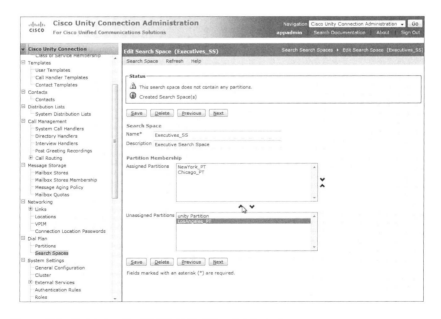

Figure 7-5   Rearrange the Partitions by Using the Arrows

Configuring User Templates in Cisco Unity Connection

Before entering large numbers of new users, you can save a lot of time by building a User Template that applies the same settings to all the newly imported users.

> **NOTE** Changes to the templates after the users have been imported have no effect on those previously imported users.

1. Using a web browser, open https://10.0.1.21/cuadmin, and enter the Application username and password.

2. Choose **Templates > User Templates**. Click the **Add New** button.

3. Enter **NewYorkEmployees** in the Alias field and **New York Employees** in the Display Name field. Leave the other settings as default, and click the **Save** button. (See Figure 7-6.)

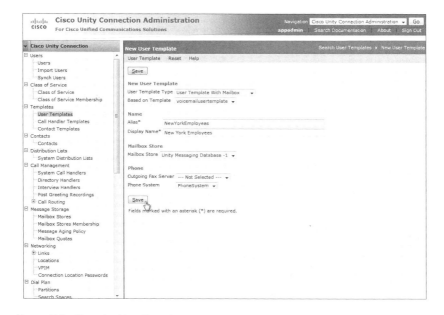

Figure 7-6 Save the User Template

4. The page refreshes with more settings available. Select **NewYork_PT** for the Partition.

5. Select **NYEmployees_SS** for the Search Scope.

6. Select **Employees_NY_COS** for the COS, and click the **Save** button. (See Figure 7-7.)

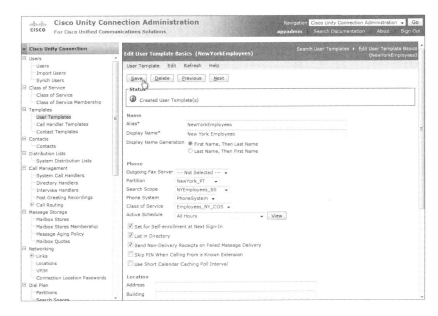

Figure 7-7 Select Additional COS Options

Managing Users in Cisco Unity Connection

There are four ways to add users to Cisco Unity Connection. Users can be added manually, by synching to a CUCM, by using LDAP, and finally by using the Bulk Administration Tool (BAT).

Adding Users Manually

Adding users manually is typically used after the system is up and running and you are just adding only a few users at a time. If you have multiple users to add, use one of the other methods here to help speed up the process and add the users in a consistent manner.

1. Using a web browser, open https://10.0.1.21/cuadmin, and enter the Application username and password.

2. Choose **Users > Users**, and then click the **Add New** button.

3. Because you already created a User Template, be sure it is selected in the **Based on Template** field. In the Alias field, enter **jsmith** and in the **Extension** field, enter **1010.** The other fields are optional, but usually you should enter the user's first and last name in the appropriate fields.

4. Click the **Save** button. The user is added and the template applied to the new user.

5. After the user is successfully created, the **Edit** menu appears. The Edit menu enables the administrator to change the password, roles, message settings, notification devices, and much more. (See Figure 7-8.)

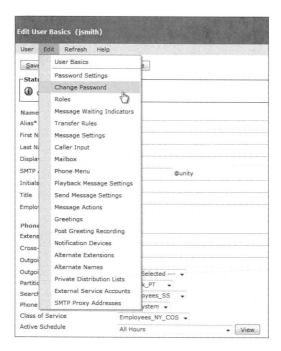

Figure 7-8   Edit Menu

Importing Users via AXL from CUCM

Users can be synched with end users that are already configured on the CUCM system using Administrative XML (AXL).

1. Make sure that the AXL service is activated. Using a web browser, open https://10.0.1.21/ccmservice, and enter the Application username and password.

2. Choose **Tools > Service Activation** and check the box next to **Cisco AXL Web Service**. Then click the **Save** button. (See Figure 7-9.)

3. Using the drop-down navigation menu on the upper right of the page, select **Cisco Unity Connection Administration**, and click the **Go** button.

4. Choose **Telephony Integrations > Phone System**. Select **PhoneSystem**; then choose **Edit > Cisco Unified Communications Manager AXL Servers**. (See Figure 7-10.)

5. Click the **Add** New button, and enter the CUCM IP Address **10.0.1.20** in the IP Address field. Then enter **8443** in the Port field.

NOTE   The username and password must be for a user that has the Standard AXL API Access role assigned in CUCM.

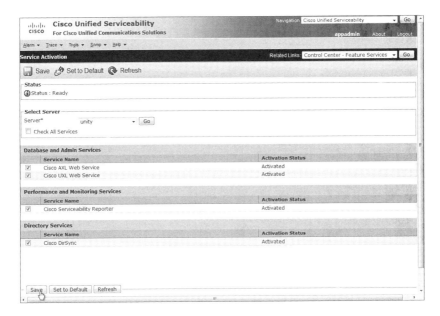

Figure 7-9   Activating Cisco AXL Web Service

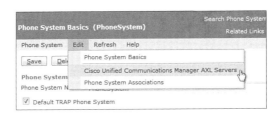

Figure 7-10   Phone System Basics Edit Menu Choices

6. Click the **Save** button. (Figure 7-11.) Click the **Test** button to ensure that the configuration is correct.

7. Choose **Users > Import Users**. Select **PhoneSystem** for the Find End Users In field, and click the **Find** button.

8. Choose **NewYorkEmployees** for the Based on Template field, and then check the boxes next to the users that were found as the search result. Click the **Import Selected** button. (See Figure 7-12.)

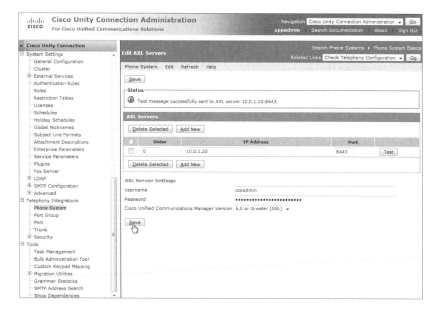

Figure 7-11   AXL Test Message Successful

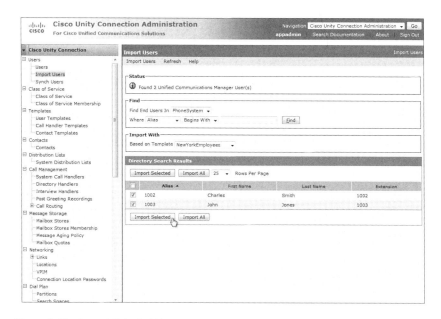

Figure 7-12   Import Selected Users

NOTE   The end users to be imported from CUCM must have a device associated
with them and also a primary extension assigned, or they will not appear in the search
results. On the End User Configuration page in CUCM in the Device Information section,

make sure there is a controlled device configured. After that is done, scroll down to the Directory Number Associations section, and select the correct DN and Partition for the Primary Extension field.

9. Now choose **Users > Users**, and click the **Find** button to verify that the users were imported correctly.

Importing Users with LDAP

Table 7-3 contains the details used when configuring LDAP on Cisco Unity Connection.

Table 7-3   LDAP Configuration

LDAP Configuration Name: Corporate LDAP	Name used in Unity Connection to iden- tify this LDAP Directory
LDAP Manager Distinguished Name: mike@voicepcg.local	User with administrative rights to LDAP
User Search Base: cn=Users, dc=voicepcg, dc=local	Defines where Unity Connection looks for users
LDAP Server Information>IP Address: 10.0.1.23	Defines the IP address of the LDAP server

1. Make sure that the Cisco DirSync service is activated. Using a web browser, open https://10.0.1.21/ccmservice, and enter the Application username and password.

2. Choose **Tools > Service Activation**, and check the box next to **Cisco DirSync** then click the **Save** button.

3. Using the drop-down navigation menu on the upper right of the page, select **Cisco Unity Connection Administration**, and click the **Go** button.

4. Choose **System Settings > LDAP > LDAP Setup**.

5. Check the box for **Enable Synchronizing from LDAP Server**, and click the **Save** button. (See Figure 7-13.)

6. Choose **System Settings > LDAP > LDAP Directory Configuration**, and click the **Add New** button.

7. In the LDAP Configuration Name field, enter **Corporate LDAP.** In the LDAP Manager Distinguished Name field, enter **mike@voicepcg** and enter the password twice below. In the LDAP User Search Base field, enter **cn=Users, dc=voicepcg, dc=local** and in the **LDAP Server Information > IP Address field**, type **10.0.1.23**.

8. Click the **Save** button. Unity Connection attempts to make a connection to the LDAP server, and if it is successful, it saves the configuration. If the connection fails, an error message displays indicating what failed. (See Figure 7-14.)

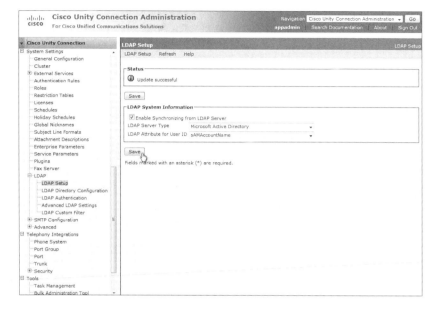

Figure 7-13   LDAP Setup

Figure 7-14   Save the LDAP Configuration

9. When the test completes and the page refreshes, click the new button labeled **Perform Full Sync Now** on the bottom. (See Figure 7-15.)

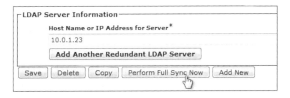

Figure 7-15   Performing an LDAP Sync

10. Choose **Users > Import Users**. In the Find End User In drop-down, select **LDAP Directory**, and click the **Find** button.

11. A list of users in LDAP will be returned. Select the **NewYorkEmployees** template. Next, check the box next to the users you would like to import, and click the **Import Selected** button. (See Figure 7-16.)

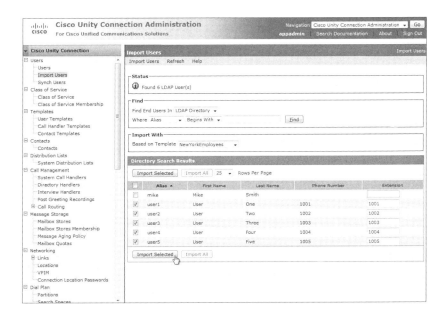

Figure 7-16   Import Users Found in LDAP

12. Choose **Users > Users** to verify that the users were imported successfully.

Importing Users with the Bulk Administration Tool (BAT)

Adding users with the Bulk Administration Tool (BAT) in Cisco Unity Connection is similar to using BAT in CUCM. There are three basic tasks that need to be done to import users using BAT in Cisco Unity Connection.

1. Select and export the comma separated value (CSV) file to your workstation.

2. Add the users to the downloaded CSV file.

3. Upload the CSV file, and import the users into Cisco Unity Connection.

NOTE   For the procedure required to add users with BAT to CUCM, see the Chapter 5, "Cisco Unified Communications Manager (CUCM) Administration and Management," section "Adding End Users and Phones with the Bulk Administration Tool (BAT)."

Following is the procedure to import users with BAT in Cisco Unity Connection:

1. Using a web browser, open https://10.0.1.21/cuadmin, and enter the Application username and password.

2. Choose **Tools > Bulk Administration Tool**.

3. In the **Select Operation** section, click the radio button next to **Export**.

4. In the **Select Object Type** section, click the radio button next to **Users with Mailbox**.

CAUTION   Updating or creating large numbers of users can negatively impact the performance of the system and should be done only during a maintenance window.

5. In the **Select File** section, type **unity_connection.csv** in the CSV File field. Click the **Submit** button. (See Figure 7-17.)

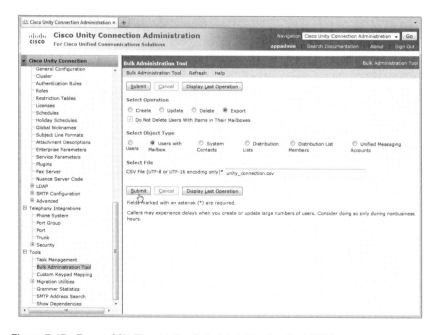

Figure 7-17   Export CSV File with the Bulk Administration Tool (BAT)

6. After the export operation finishes, the Status area at the top of the page generates a link that you can use to download the file. Click **Download the Export File.** (See Figure 7-18.)

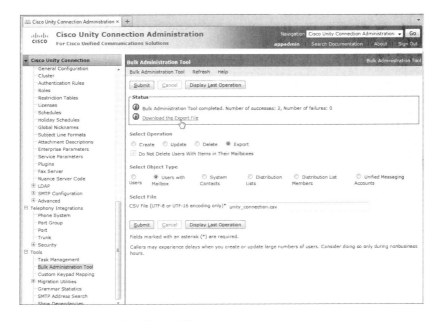

Figure 7-18   Download the Export File

7. Open the downloaded file with Microsoft Excel or other software that can edit the CSV file. There are many columns to fill in, but just use the following six columns: Alias, FirstName, LastName, DisplayName, Extension, and ListInDirectory. The column letters are included in Figure 7-19, and other columns are hidden that you are not using right now. Add the users as indicated here, and save the edited CSV file.

	A	O	R	Y	AV
1	Alias	FirstName	LastName	Extension	ListInDirectory
2	user1	User	One	1005	1
3	user2	User	Two	1006	1
4	user3	User	Three	1007	1
5	user4	User	Four	1008	1
6					

Figure 7-19   Complete the Columns with User Information

8. Using a web browser, open https://10.0.1.21/cuadmin, and enter the Application username and password.

9. Choose **Tools > Bulk Administration Tool**.

10. In the **Select Operation** section, click the radio button next to **Update**.

11. In the **Select Object Type** section, click the radio button next to **Users with Mailbox**.

12. In the **User Template** section, click the radio button next to **Yes**, and select **NewYorkEmployees** in the drop-down menu.

13. In the **Select File** section, type **unity_connection.csv** in the CSV File field. In the **Failed Objects Filename** field, type **failed.csv**. Click the **Submit** button. (See Figure 7-20.)

Figure 7-20   Upload the BAT File to Import the Users

14. A status section appears and shows the progress of the import. (See Figure 7-21.) After the operation is complete, you can then choose **Users > Users** to verify that the users were indeed imported. (See Figure 7-22.)

Figure 7-21   BAT Import Successful

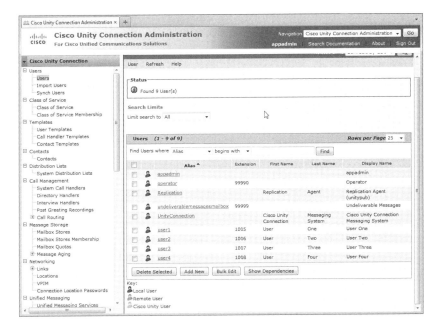

Figure 7-22   Verifying That the Users Were Imported

Configuring Call Handlers in Cisco Unity Connection

A call handler can serve multiple functions in Cisco Unity Connection. A call handler can answer calls, take messages, be part of an auto-attendant, play a recorded announcement, and transfer calls to users or other call handlers.

In this example, you create a call handler with which a user can press 0 to go to the operator and press 9 for the directory.

1. Using a web browser, open https://10.0.1.21/cuadmin, and enter the Application username and password.

2. Choose **Call Management > System Call Handlers.** Click the **Add New** button.

3. Enter **Main_Menu_CH** in the Display Name field.

TIP   You can enter a name followed by some indication of what the name refers to. For example, here you can use **Main_Menu_CH** for Main Menu Call Handler. If you are making a new Partition, use **Menu_PT** to indicate it is a Menu Partition. Appending a descriptor such as _CH or _PT helps when reviewing traces and log files to identify configured items.

4. Type **5000** in the Extension field, and click the **Save** button.

5. Select **NewYork_PT** for the Partition, and click the **Play/Record** button to record the Main Menu. Click the **Save** button. (See Figure 7-23.)

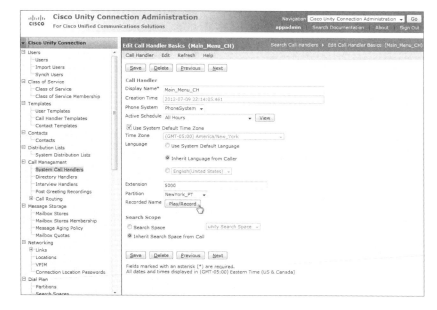

Figure 7-23   Record the Main Menu

6. Choose **Edit > Caller Input**. (See Figure 7-24.)

Figure 7-24   Edit the Caller Menu Options

7. Select the 0 key. (See Figure 7-25.)

8. Select the radio button next to **Call Handler**, and select **Operator** from the menu. When users dial 0 from the menu, they will be connected to the operator. Attempt transfer means that the system will transfer the call to the operator's phone. If you choose Go Directly to Greetings, the operator will not have a chance to answer the call, and the operator's greeting starts playing.

9. Click the **Save** button. (See Figure 7-26.)

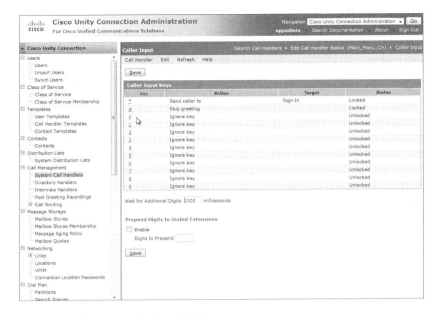

Figure 7-25   Change the Options for "0"

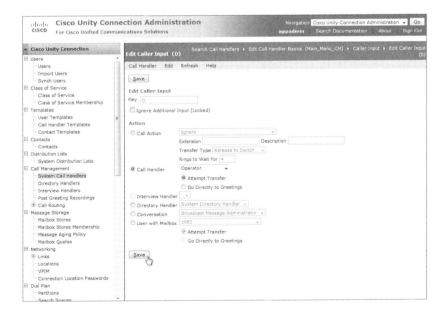

Figure 7-26   Transfer to the Operator Call Handler

10. Choose **Edit > Caller Input**. Select the 9 key. This is the Directory Key.

11. Select the radio button next to **Directory Handler**, and select **System Directory Handler**. Then click the **Save** button.

12. Choose **Edit > Greetings**. There are multiple greetings available. (See Figure 7-27.)

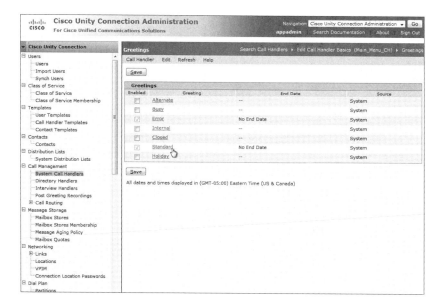

Figure 7-27   Greetings

Table 7-4 provides details about how the greetings are used and what greetings override other greetings.

Table 7-4   Greeting Descriptions

Greeting Type	Greeting Override?	Description
Alternate	Overrides all other greetings	Useful for special situations like out of office for an extended period of time.
Busy	Overrides standard, internal, closed, and holiday greetings	Plays when the target's extension is busy.
Error	None	Plays when a caller enters invalid digits in a call handler/mailbox.
Internal	Overrides standard, closed, and holiday greetings	This greeting is for internal callers and tends to be more informal or adds information that only internal callers need to know like, "I am in the Sales Meeting in Room 1776 today."

Greeting Type	Greeting Override?	Description
Closed	Overrides standard greeting	Plays when the business is closed according to the active schedule.
Standard	None	Plays when not overridden by another greeting.
Holiday	Overrides the standard and closed greeting	Plays when the business is closed for a holiday as specified in the active schedule's holiday dates.

13. Select the **Standard** greeting, and record a message for callers indicating that they can dial 0 for the operator or 9 for the directory. Click the **Save** button.

14. Choose **Edit > Message Settings**. Uncheck **Callers Can Edit Messages**, and change the Message Recipient to **User with Mailbox**. Then select **user5**. Click the **Save** button. (See Figure 7-28.)

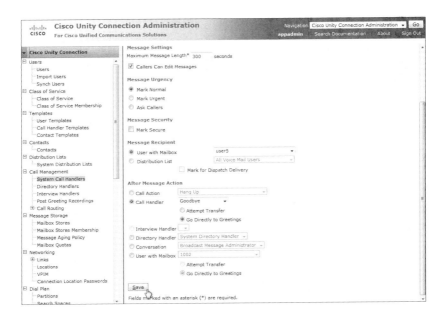

Figure 7-28 Save Call Handler Message Settings

15. Choose the owner of the call handler to administer the greetings and other settings. Choose **Edit > Call Handler Owners**, and click the **Add User** button. A new window opens with the users available to be the call handler owner. Check **jsmith** and click **Add Selected User**. Then click the **Close** button. (See Figure 7-29.)

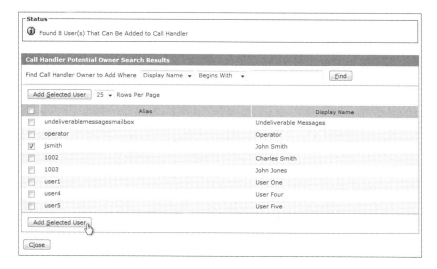

Figure 7-29　Add Selected User

Cisco Unity Connection Reports

Cisco Unity Connection includes many built-in reports that you can run to monitor and troubleshoot the system.

1. Using a web browser, open https://10.0.1.21/cuservice, and enter the Application username and password.

2. Choose **Tools > Reports**. (See Figure 7-30.)

The reports can be viewed as a web page, comma-separated value (CSV) or PDF.

Figure 7-30　Unity Connection Report List

Cisco Unified Presence Server Administration Interfaces

The Cisco Unified Presence Server uses CUCM for user administration.

Table 7-5   Cisco Unified Presence Server Administration Interfaces

Administration Interface	Access Method	Username/Password Combo
Cisco Unified Presence Administration	https://<IPAddress>/cupadmin	Application Username/Password
Cisco Unified Serviceability	https://<IPAddress>/ccmservice	Application Username/Password
Cisco Unified OS Administration	https://<IPAddress>/cmplatform	Platform Username/Password
Disaster Recovery System	https://<IPAddress>/drf	Platform Username/Password
Cisco Unified Reporting	https://<IPAddress>/cucreports	Application Username/Password
Command Line Interface	SSH to <IPAddress>	Platform Username/Password
End User Web Access	https://<IPAddress>/cupuser	End UserID /Password

NOTE   There is a web interface for end users to access their presence setting and manage their account.

Cisco Unity Connection and Cisco Unified Presence Backup and Restore

The Backup and Restore functionality in Cisco Unity Connection and Cisco Unified Presence is the same as CUCM, which is covered in Chapter 8, "Management, Monitoring, and Troubleshooting CUCM" in the "Configuring Backup and Recovery" section. Refer to that chapter and section for details on backup and restore configuration.

Management, Monitoring, and Troubleshooting CUCM

This chapter provides information and commands concerning the following topics:

- Cisco IP Phone boot and restart processes
  - Cisco IP Phone boot process
  - Phone restart procedure
  - Troubleshooting using the phone web page
- Dialed Number Analyzer
- Cisco Unified Reporting
- Cisco Real Time Monitoring Tool (RTMT)
- Monitoring and troubleshooting using CLI commands
- Configuring backup and recovery

Topology

The topology in Figure 8-1 will be used for troubleshooting and monitoring Cisco Unified Voice.

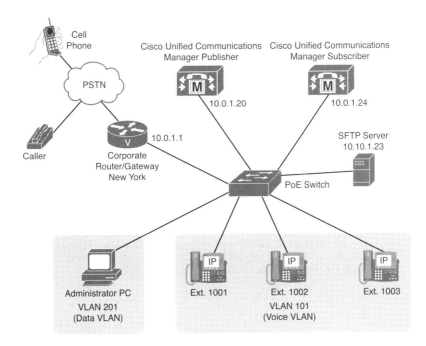

Figure 8-1 Topology

Cisco IP Phone Boot and Restart Processes

Following are the processes required to boot and restart the Cisco IP Phone.

Cisco IP Phone Boot Process

Knowing the Cisco IP Phone boot process can help troubleshoot phone registration problems and connectivity issues. Some phone models display more information than others during the boot phase. The 79XX series phones typically show more boot information than the 69XX series phones, for instance. See Table 8-1 for a listing of the phone boot process.

Table 8-1 Phone Boot Process

Power Is Provided	The phone can obtain power from a Power over Ethernet (PoE) switch, power supply, or an inline power injector.
Firmware Loaded	The phone loads stored firmware from flash memory.
VLAN Configured	If the phone is connected to a Cisco switch and a voice VLAN is configured for that interface, the switch informs the phone which VLAN to use for voice traffic.
IP Address and TFTP Server Address Obtained	An IP address is configured using DHCP. The DHCP server provides a list of TFTP server IP addresses using DHCP option 150. **NOTE** DHCP option 66 gives the IP address of a single TFTP server.
Configuration Files Retrieved	The phone contacts the TFTP server and requests its configuration file named SEP <is MAC of Phone>.cnf.xml. That file includes the IP address of the CUCM server that the phone should register with.
Registration with CUCM	The phone registers with the correct CUCM.

See Figure 8-2 for a diagram of the boot process and components.

NOTE It is a best practice to have separate and redundant DHCP and TFTP servers on the network. However, for smaller deployments, the CUCM can also act as both DHCP and TFTP servers as well for simplified management.

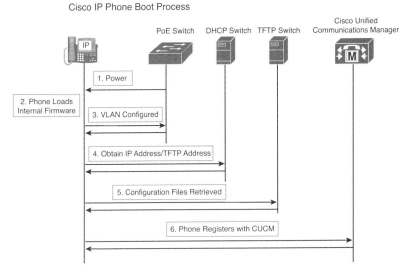

Cisco IP Phone Boot Process

Figure 8-2   Boot Process and Components

Phone Restart Procedure

To restart most Cisco IP phones, press the **Settings** button and then ****#**** on the keypad.

Troubleshooting Using the Phone Web Page

Many factors can affect VoIP call quality and call completion. The CUCM includes some tools to help troubleshoot these factors to help narrow the field of possibilities. One of the most useful troubleshooting tools is the phone. When a user complains about poor call quality, you can use the phone's built-in web server to view real-time statistics.

1. Using a web browser, open https://10.0.1.20/ccmadmin, and enter the Application username and password.

2. Choose **Device > Phone**. Click the **Find** button.

3. Locate the phone that you would like to troubleshoot. Click the hyperlink for the IP address. (See Figure 8-3.)

4. A new window opens with the web page from the phone. If no web page opens, go to the Device Information page for the phone, and ensure that **Web Access** is set to **Enabled**.

5. The page displays a wealth of information such as MAC address, Firmware Version, Phone DN, Phone Type, and whether the Message Waiting Lamp is lit. (See Figure 8-4.)

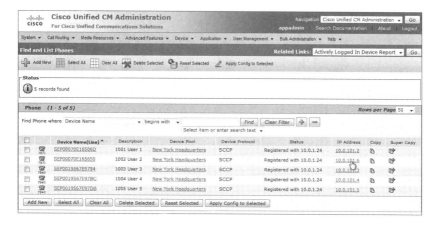

Figure 8-3   Choose the Device by Its IP Address

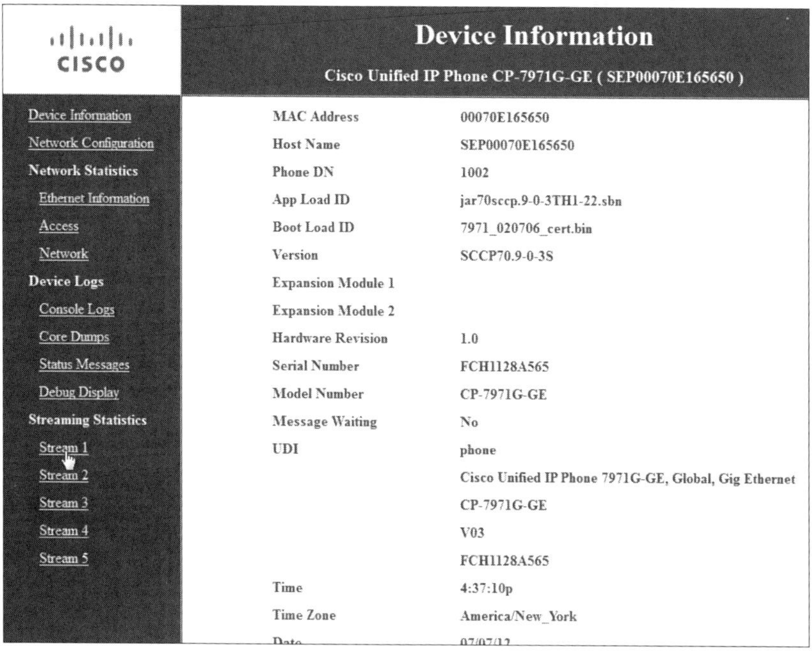

Figure 8-4   Device Web Page

6. Choose **Network Statistics > Network**. On this page, you can scroll down to find the switch name and port number that the phone is connected to. This information greatly simplifies locating the connection in the LAN room for troubleshooting. (See Figure 8-5.)

NOTE   The switch name and port are determined using the Cisco Discovery Protocol (CDP) and work only with devices that support CDP.

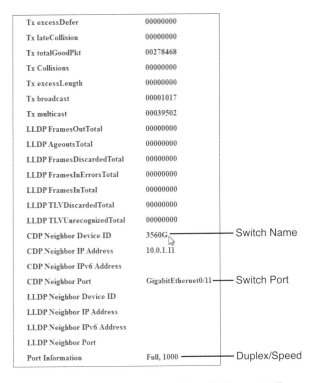

Tx excessDefer	00000000
Tx lateCollision	00000000
Tx totalGoodPkt	00278468
Tx Collisions	00000000
Tx excessLength	00000000
Tx broadcast	00001017
Tx multicast	00039502
LLDP FramesOutTotal	00000000
LLDP AgeoutsTotal	00000000
LLDP FramesDiscardedTotal	00000000
LLDP FramesInErrorsTotal	00000000
LLDP FramesInTotal	00000000
LLDP TLVDiscardedTotal	00000000
LLDP TLVUnrecognizedTotal	00000000
CDP Neighbor Device ID	3560G
CDP Neighbor IP Address	10.0.1.11
CDP Neighbor IPv6 Address	
CDP Neighbor Port	GigabitEthernet0/11
LLDP Neighbor Device ID	
LLDP Neighbor IP Address	
LLDP Neighbor IPv6 Address	
LLDP Neighbor Port	
Port Information	Full, 1000

Switch Name — CDP Neighbor Device ID 3560G
Switch Port — CDP Neighbor Port GigabitEthernet0/11
Duplex/Speed — Port Information Full, 1000

Figure 8-5   View the Switch Name and Port the Phone Is Connected To

7. If the user complains about call quality, you can have the user place a call and view some real-time statistics. Choose **Streaming Statistics > Stream 1** and view the counters for Latency, Jitter, and Packet Loss.

Dialed Number Analyzer

The Dialed Number Analyzer verifies call routing when troubleshooting call completion issues or building your dial plan. Using the dialed digits, Calling Search Space, and DN, the Dialed Number Analyzer tool can show the applicable matched route pattern and alternative routing options, if any, that the CUCM considered when making a routing decision.

Because the Dialed Number Analyzer is not activated by default, you must first activate the service.

1. Using a web browser, open https://10.0.1.20/ccmservice, and enter the Application username and password.

2. Choose **Tools > Service Activation**. Select **10.0.1.20** and click the **Go** button.

3. Check the box next to **Cisco Dialed Number Analyzer** and click the **Save** button. (See Figure 8-6.)

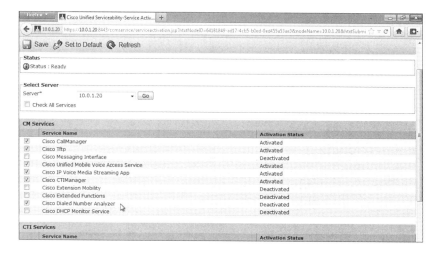

Figure 8-6   Enable the Dialed Number Analyzer Service

4. Refresh the browser page so that the Dialed Number Analyzer menu item appears under the **Tools** menu.

5. Choose **Tools > Dialed Number Analyzer**.

6. Choose **Analysis > Analyzer.**

7. Enter **1001** in the Calling Party field and **92125551212** in the Dialed Digits field. Select the **Employees_CSS** Calling Search Space, and click the **Do Analysis** button. (See Figure 8-7.)

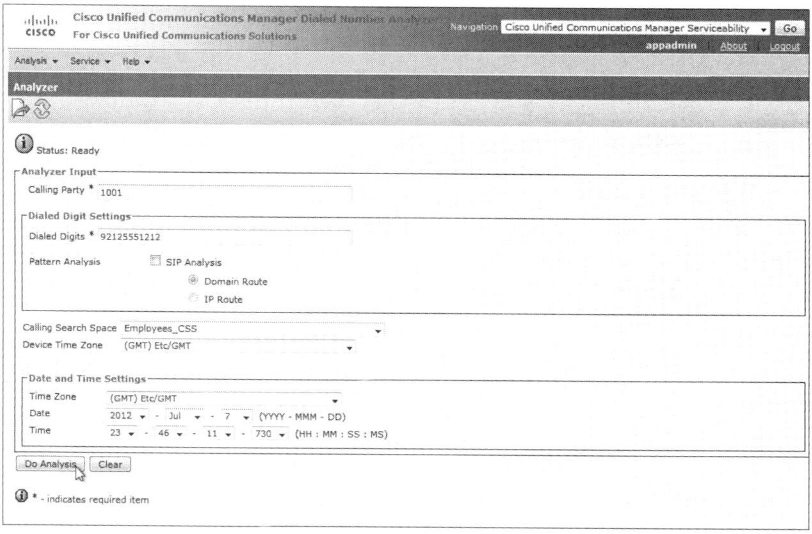

Figure 8-7   Enter Details for Analysis

8. In this example, the call is blocked because long distance dialing is not enabled for the Employees_CSS Calling Search Space. (See Figure 8-8.)

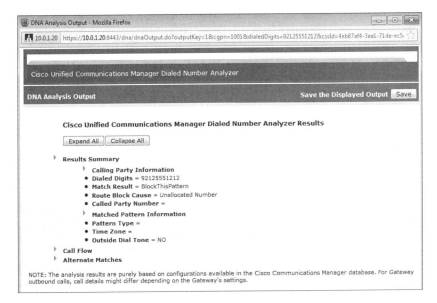

Figure 8-8   The Result Indicates That the Call Is Blocked

9. Change the Dialed Digits field to **95551212** and note how the result changes and now the End Device is chosen (10.0.1.1 is the gateway.) (See Figure 8-9.)

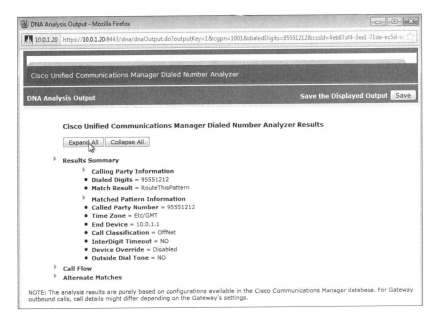

Figure 8-9   The Result Indicates That the Call Is Routed

TIP   Click the **Expand All** button for a detailed view of the call flow.

Cisco Unified Reporting

The built-in reports that Cisco provides are a great way to gather a great deal of information in an easy-to-read and exportable format.

1. Using a web browser, open https://10.0.1.20/cucreports, and enter the Application username and password.

2. Choose **System Reports**.

3. To get a description of the built-in reports, click the **Report Descriptions** link, and then click the **Generate a New Report** link. (See Figure 8-10.)

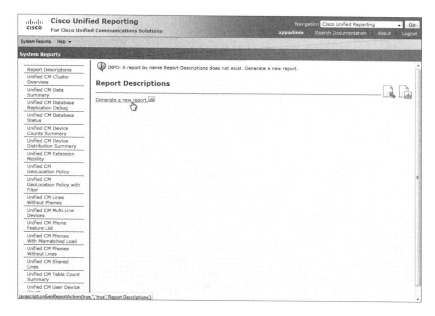

Figure 8-10   Click to Generate a New Report

4. The result lists a detailed description of the reports available and symptoms and remedies. (See Figure 8-11.)

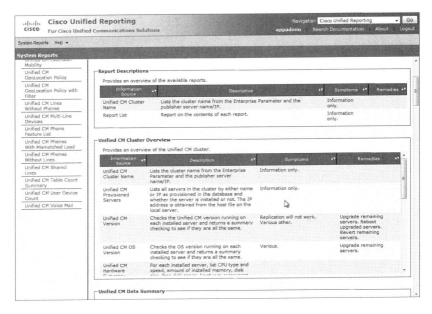

Figure 8-11 Listing of Report Descriptions and Symptoms

Cisco Real Time Monitoring Tool (RTMT)

The Cisco Real Time Monitoring Tool is an application included with the CUCM that provides real-time information on the status and health of your system.

First, you must download and install the RTMT.

1. Using a web browser, open https://10.0.1.20/ccmadmin, and enter the Application username and password.

2. Choose **Application > Plugins**. Click the **Find** button. Scroll down to find the Cisco Real Time Monitoring Tool link and download for the appropriate operating system that the tool will be running on. Install the application as you would normally. (See Figure 8-12.)

Figure 8-12   Download and Install RTMT

3. Log in using the Application username and password. (See Figure 8-13.)

Figure 8-13   Use the Application Administrator Credentials with RTMT

There are three menu areas to choose from: System, CallManager, and AnalysisManager. Following are the views that are most useful for monitoring and troubleshooting:

- **System > System Summary:** Virtual Memory Usage, CPU Usage, Common Partition Usage, and Alert History for the cluster. (See Figure 8-14.)

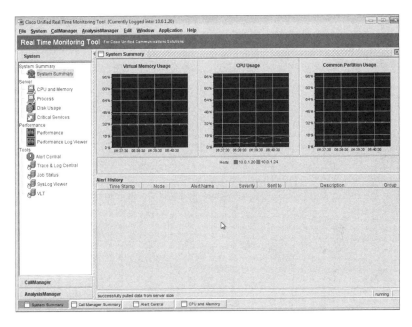

Figure 8-14   System > System Summary

■ **System > Tools > Alert Central:** Overview of system alarms. You can leave this open all day. (See Figure 8-15.)

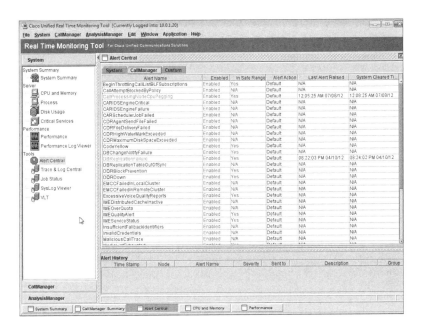

Figure 8-15   System > Tools > Alert Central

■ **System > Tools > SysLog Viewer:** Select the node and choose **Application Logs > Alternate Syslog** for information about phone registrations. (See Figure 8-16.)

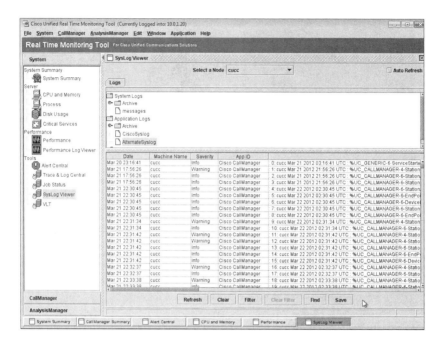

Figure 8-16   System > Tools > SysLog Viewer

■ **CallManager > CallManagerSummary:** Registered Phones and Calls in Progress; useful for viewing system activity before performing maintenance.

■ **CallManager > CallProcess > Call Activity:** Before performing any maintenance, check this view and the CallManagerSummary view to verify that there are no active calls. (See Figure 8-17.)

■ **CallManager > Device > Device Summary:** Overview of registered phones, FXS, FXO, T1CAS, PRI, MOH, MTP, and CFB devices. After you get your system running and stabilized, it is a good idea to monitor this view for changes. (See Figure 8-18.)

■ **CallManager > Device > Device Search:** Provides detailed information about device status. The reports are in a table format and can be sorted by column. (See Figure 8-19.)

TIP   For detailed graphs and real-time troubleshooting, you can choose **System > Performance > Performance**, and choose from many items to monitor relating to the health of the system.

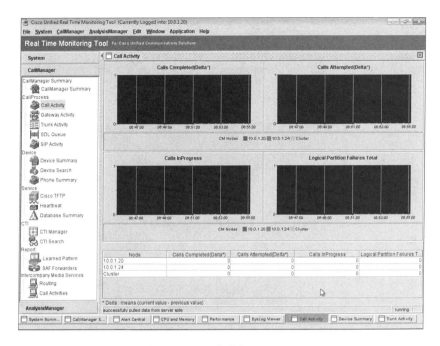

Figure 8-17 CallManager > CallProcess > Call Activity

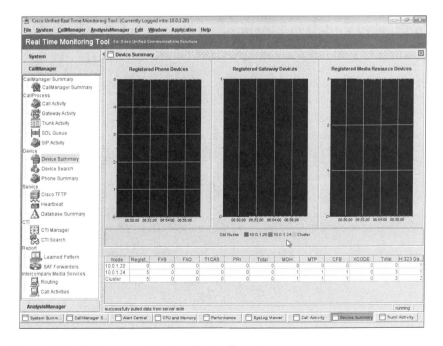

Figure 8-18 CallManager > Device > Device Summary

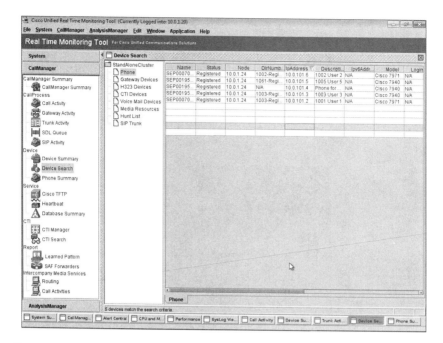

Figure 8-19   CallManager > Device > Device Search.

Monitoring and Troubleshooting Using CLI Commands

Log in to the CLI using the operating system username and password.

> **CAUTION**   Be careful when using CLI commands because few actually prompt you with an Are You Sure message before executing the command.

Table 8-2   CLI Commands

admin:?	Shows available commands.
admin:**help <command>**	Help for a command.
admin:**show version active**	Displays active system version.
admin:**show version inactive**	Displays if there are any other alternative versions installed. This is used when an upgrade is performed.
admin:**utils service list**	Displays a list of services and their status.
admin:**show tech all**	Displays useful information for Cisco TAC.
admin:**utils network ping <IPAddress>**	Pings an address and displays result.
admin:**utils network traceroute <IPAddress>**	Performs a traceroute to an IP address and displays the result.

admin:utils reset_application_ ui_administrator_password	Resets the Application password.
admin:utils reset_application_ ui_administrator_name	Resets the Application username.
admin:utils reset_ui_ administrator_password	Resets the operating system administrator password.
admin:utils reset_ui_ administrator_name	Resets the operating system administrator's username.
admin:utils system shutdown	Powers off the system
admin:utils system restart	Restarts the system.
admin:utils system switch-version	If another version of CUCM has been loaded on the system, this command allows you to switch to it. This is used during upgrades so that if there is a problem with an upgraded version, you can easily revert back to the previous version.
admin:utils system upgrade {cancel	initiate	status}	Used to initiate, cancel, or get a status of a system upgrade being performed either locally or via a remote filesystem.
admin:show environment {fans	power-supply	temperatures}	Useful in monitoring the hardware for temperature, fan speed, and power-supply information.
admin:quit	Logs you out and ends the management session.

Configuring Backup and Recovery

The built-in backup and recovery operation uses either a Secure File Transfer Protocol (SFTP) server or tape device. If you use SFTP, you need to make sure that the CUCM has access to the SFTP server through the network and obtain a username and password on the SFTP server for the CUCM to use to perform backups. The backups consist of the configuration and user data but not the operating system or patches applied.

1. Using a web browser, open https://10.0.1.20/drf, and enter the operating system username and password.

2. Choose **Backup > Backup Device**. Click the **Add New** button.

3. Enter **SFTP_Server** in the Backup device name field. Add the IP address, pathname, username, and password in the appropriate fields, and click the **Save** button. The CUCM attempts to log in to the SFTP server to test connectivity. If the test succeeds, the page updates with Update Successful at the top of the web page. If the test fails, the SFTP is not added, and you must try again. (See Figure 8-20.)

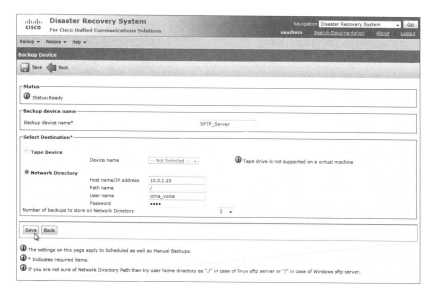

Figure 8-20   Configure a Backup Device

4. Create a schedule to perform backups on a regular basis. Choose **Backup >
   Scheduler**, and click the **Add New** button. Choose from the available options and
   click the **Save** button.

5. After the update is successful, be sure to choose the **Enable Schedule** button to
   activate the scheduled backup.

NOTE   You can view the history of backups by choosing **Backup > History**.

TIP   To perform a system restore, choose **Restore > Restore Wizard**.

Summary

The CUCM includes many built-in reports that you should explore to gain more insight
into how your system operates and to help with maintenance and management activities. The Real Time Monitoring Tool is a great way to view alerts and gather real-time
information about your system that would be difficult to get otherwise. Take some time
to become familiar with the included reports and tools so that when trouble does arise,
you'll know where to look to begin troubleshooting.

CHAPTER 9

Putting It All Together

This chapter provides an outline of steps to complete to implement a Cisco Voice solution using Cisco Unified Communications Manager and Cisco Unified Communications Manager Express. Use this outline to verify your understanding of the CCNA Voice concepts and configuration in a real-world scenario.

- Topology
- Have You Completed These Steps?
  - Design
  - Configuration
  - Verification
  - Troubleshooting

Topology

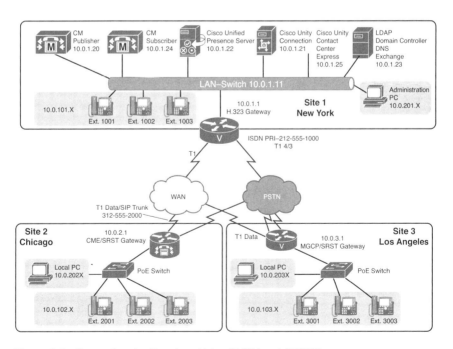

Figure 9-1 Comprehensive Topology Using CUCM and CUCME

Design

✓	Design the IP Address scheme using your CCNA knowledge for voice and data.
✓	Define the DHCP scopes to be used for both data and voice.
✓	Design the Voice Dial Plan.
✓	Will there be a secondary dial-tone digit? If so, define it.

Configuration

✓	Physically connect the fundamental devices.			
✓	Configure the routers.			
	✓	Hostname		
	✓	Interfaces		
	✓	Physical		
	✓	Subinterfaces		
✓	Configure the switches.			
	✓	Hostname		
	✓	MGMT VLAN interface		
	✓	Interfaces		
		✓	IEEE 802.1q trunk	
		✓	Voice only	
		✓	Data only	
		✓	Voice and data	
✓	Reset the IP Phones to factory defaults.			
✓	Configure one or more of the routers as NTP servers.			
✓	Configure one or more of the routers as DHCP servers.			
✓	Configure the CUCME routers for telephony.			
✓	Configure the CUCME routers for			
	✓	SCCP and SIP.		
	✓	The maximum number of phones.		
	✓	The maximum number of extensions.		
	✓	The typical date format used in the USA.		
	✓	The 12-hour time format.		
	✓	Enable hook flash.		
	✓	Display a message on the phones.		
	✓	The directory naming schema should be Last Name First.		
	✓	Specify a Music-On-Hold .au or .wav file.		
	✓	Override Phone PIN.		

	✓	System username and password for web administration.
	✓	Customer username and password for web access.
	✓	The interval between subsequent digits entered should be 20 seconds.
	✓	A dialplan pattern with tag information to be expanded to E.164 numbers.
	✓	A transfer pattern for non-Cisco IP Phones.
	✓	Custom Phone URLs.
	✓	User accounts with customized options.
	✓	Make sure to modify at least one user account.
	✓	Endpoint creation.
	✓	Make sure to modify at least one endpoint.
	✓	Create directory numbers.
	✓	Make sure to modify at least one directory number.
	✓	Define calling privileges.
	✓	Define user features such as
		✓ Calling privileges
		✓ Extension mobility
		✓ Call coverage
		✓ Intercom
		✓ Native presence
	✓	Unified mobility remote destination.
✓	Configure CUCM for	
	✓	Change the CUCM name to an IP Address for DNS independence.
	✓	Create a Unified CM Group.
	✓	Create a Phone NTP Reference (for SIP phones only).
	✓	A Date/Time Group.
	✓	Locations.
	✓	Device Pools.
	✓	Create a Partition.
	✓	Create a Call Search Space.
	✓	Activate Services and Features.
	✓	Create a Phone Button template.
	✓	Create a Softkey template.
	✓	Create a Common Phone Profile.
	✓	Create an Application User with Administrative Rights.
	✓	Create an Application User with Read-Only Rights.
	✓	Create an end user manually.

	✓	Add users via LDAP Synchronization.
	✓	LDAP Authentication for end users.
	✓	Add an IP Phone manually.
	✓	Add a Directory Number (DN) to a phone.
	✓	Add phones using Auto-registration.
	✓	Add end users and phones with the Bulk Administration Tool (BAT).
	✓	Add an H.323 and MGCP Gateway.
	✓	Create a Route Group.
	✓	Create a Route List.
	✓	Create a Route Pattern.
	✓	Hunt Groups.
	✓	Shared Lines.
	✓	Barge and Privacy.
	✓	Call Forwarding.
	✓	Call Pickup.
	✓	Call Park.
	✓	Directed Call Park.
	✓	Native Presence.
	✓	Extension Mobility.
	✓	Intercom.
	✓	Mobile Connect.
	✓	Mobile Voice Access.
✓	Configure Cisco Unity Connection for	
	✓	Class of Service.
	✓	Partitions.
	✓	Search Spaces.
	✓	User Templates.
	✓	Add a user manually.
	✓	Import users via AXL from CUCM.
	✓	Import users with LDAP.
	✓	Import users with BAT.
	✓	Connection Reports.
✓	Configure Unified Presence with basic parameters.	
✓	Configure Backup and Recovery.	

Verification

✓	Using various show commands and graphical utilities, verify everything is working correctly.	
	✓	Can you make calls?
	✓	Can you receive calls?
	✓	Can you retrieve voicemail?
	✓	Can you use the intercom?
	✓	Can you transfer a call?
	✓	Can you... ? (Think about other questions you should be asking.)

Troubleshooting

✓	Using various debug commands and graphical utilities, troubleshoot any potential problems within the voice infrastructure.

APPENDIX

Create Your Own Journal Here

Even though we have tried to be as complete as possible in this reference guide, invariably we might have left something out that you need in your specific day-to-day activities. That is why this section is here. Use these blank lines to enter your own notes, making this reference guide your own personalized journal.

_____

_____

_____

_____

_____

_____

_____

_____

_____

_____

_____

_____

_____

_____

_____